Advanced Practical Organic Chemistry

Dedicated to Professor Gilbert Stork
In recognition of the skills and enthusiasm for chemistry
gained in his laboratories

ADVANCED PRACTICAL
ORGANIC CHEMISTRY

M. CASEY
J. LEONARD
B. LYGO
Department of Chemistry and Applied Chemistry
University of Salford
G. PROCTER
George Ramage Professor of Chemistry
University of Salford

BLACKIE ACADEMIC & PROFESSIONAL
An Imprint of Chapman & Hall
London · Glasgow · New York · Tokyo · Melbourne · Madras

Published by Blackie Academic & Professional, an imprint of
Chapman & Hall, Wester Cleddens Road, Bishopbriggs, Glasgow
G64 2NZ, UK

Chapman & Hall, 2-6 Boundary Row, London SE1 8HN, UK

Blackie Academic & Professional, Wester Cleddens Road,
Bishopbriggs, Glasgow G64 2NZ, UK

Chapman & Hall, 29 West 35th Street, New York NY10001, USA

Chapman & Hall Japan, Thomson Publishing Japan, Hirakawacho
Nemoto Building, 6F, 1-7-11 Hirakawa-cho, Chiyoda-ku, Tokyo 102,
Japan

DA Book (Aust.) Pty Ltd, 648 Whitehorse Road, Mitcham 3132,
Victoria, Australia

Chapman & Hall India, R. Seshadri, 32 Second Main Road, CIT East,
Madras 600 035, India

First edition 1990
Reprinted 1993

© 1990 Blackie Academic & Professional

Printed in Great Britain by Thomson Litho Ltd, Scotland

ISBN 0 7514 0140 4

A catalogue record for this book is available from the British Library
Library of Congress Cataloging-in-Publication Data available

Preface

The preparation of organic compounds is central to many areas of scientific research, from the most applied to the most academic, and is not limited to chemists. Any research which uses new organic chemicals, or those which are not available commercially, will at some time require the synthesis of such compounds.

This highly practical book, covering the most up-to-date techniques commonly used in organic synthesis, is based on our experience of establishing research groups in synthetic organic chemistry and our association with some of the leading laboratories in the field. It is not claimed to be a comprehensive compilation of information to meet all possible needs and circumstances; rather, the intention has been to provide sufficient guidance to allow the researcher to carry out reactions under conditions which offer the highest chance of success.

The book is written for postgraduate and advanced level undergraduate organic chemists and for chemists in industry, particularly those involved in pharmaceutical, agrochemical and other fine chemicals research. Biologists, biochemists, genetic engineers, material scientists and polymer researchers in university and industry will find the book a useful source of reference.

Contents

CHAPTER 1

General Introduction

The preparation of organic compounds is central to many areas of scientific research, from the most applied to the most academic, and is not limited to chemists alone. Any research which uses new organic chemicals, or those which are not available commercially, will at some time require the synthesis of such compounds. Accordingly the biologist, biochemist, genetic engineer, materials scientist, and polymer researcher in university or industry all might find themselves faced with the task of carrying out an organic preparation, along with those involved in pharmaceutical, agrochemical, and other fine chemicals research.

These scientists share with the new organic chemistry graduate student a need to be able to carry out modern organic synthesis with confidence and in such a way as to maximize the chance of success. The techniques, methods, and reagents used in organic synthesis are numerous, and increasing every year. Many of these demand particular conditions and care at several stages of the process, and it is unrealistic to expect an undergraduate course to prepare the chemist for all the situations which might be met in the research laboratories. The non-specialist is even more likely not to be conversant with most modern techniques and reagents.

Nevertheless, it is perfectly possible for both the non-specialist and the graduate student beginning research in organic chemistry to carry out such reactions with success, provided that the appropriate precautions are taken and the proper experimental protocol is observed.

Much of this is common sense, given a knowledge of the properties of the reagents being used, as most general techniques are relatively straightforward. However, it is often very difficult for the beginner or non-specialist to find the appropriate information.

At Salford, we found ourselves handing out to students beginning research in organic chemistry a compilation of what we hoped was useful information on the practical aspects of organic synthesis, based on the authors' recent associations with some of the top synthetic organic research laboratories. We have gathered this information together in this book, and expanded it to cover some other areas, in the hope that it will be an aid to the specialists and non-specialists alike. Of course most research groups will have their own modifications and requirements, but on the whole the basic principles will remain the same.

This book is intended to be a guide to carrying out the types of reactions which are widely used in modern organic synthesis, and is concerned with basic technique. It is not intended to be a comprehensive survey of reagents and methods. A few representative procedures are given, and the appendix contains some information on commonly used reagents.

If we have achieved our aims, users of this book should be able to approach their synthetic tasks with confidence. Organic synthesis is both exciting and satisfying, and provides opportunity for real creativity. If our book helps anyone along this particular path then our efforts will have been worthwhile.

CHAPTER 2

Keeping Records of Laboratory Work

2.1 Introduction

No matter how high the standard of experimental technique employed during a reaction, the results will be of little use unless an accurate record is kept of how that reaction was carried out and of the data obtained on the product(s). Individuals or individual research groups will develop their own style for recording experimental data, but no matter what format you choose to follow, there are certain pieces of vital information which should always be included. In this section a format for keeping records of experimental data will be suggested and although this need not be strictly adhered to, it will be used to point out the essential features which should be included. It is suggested that records of experimental work and experimental data be kept in two complementary forms: *The lab notebook* should be a diary of experiments performed and should contain exact details of how experiments were carried out; A *data book* or set of *data sheets* should also be kept to record the physical data and preferred experimental procedure for each individual compound which has been synthesized.

2.2 The laboratory notebook

2.2.1 Why keep a lab book ?

Before any practical work is undertaken in the laboratory a sturdy hard-backed lab notebook should be obtained and a standard format for keeping the notebook should be decided upon. A good deal of thought should go into the layout of the lab book. It should be stressed that a lab book is not a format for polished report writing, but a daily log of work carried out in the lab. Some of the main reasons for keeping a lab book are:

1. In order that the exact procedure followed for a reaction can be referred to later. This can be very important even if the reaction was not successful. For instance, after several attempts to bring about a reaction have failed, it is often possible to review what has been done then carry out a more successful experiment.

2. It should be the main index point that will enable you to find experimental, literature and spectroscopic data on any compound which you have synthesized.

3. It is the main source of reference when you come to write reports, papers, theses etc.

4. It is a chronological diary of the experiments carried out and thus it should allow you to say exactly when a particular experiment was carried out.

5. In order that another worker can follow your work, it is very important to use a lab book style which is easily understood by others.

2.2.2 How to write a lab book

One of the most important points about keeping a lab book is that it is kept on the bench and written up as you perform the experiments. *It is bad practice to keep rough notes about experiments, then transfer the details to a lab book later.* This can cause many problems, for instance: the original notes can be lost; even with the strongest will, the exact truth often becomes distorted in transferring information to the lab book and small facts which may at the time seem unimportant are left out; it is also very easy to forget to rewrite an experiment altogether, especially if the reaction failed, and this can lead to much time wasting later. It is more important that the lab book be an accurate record of the way an experiment was performed, than for it to be in your neatest writing, although of course it should be legible.

An example of a format that is effective for general synthetic chemistry is outlined on page 6. This can be adjusted to personal needs but its essential features, which are listed below, should be included in any format chosen.

2.2.3 Suggested notebook format (Fig. 2.1)

1. General layout

It is good practice to start each new experiment on the next free right hand page of the notebook. This makes finding any particular experiment easier.

2. Experiment number

The experiment number is in the top right hand corner of the page and this is very important since it is used to reference all the compounds which are prepared. If a notebook with numbered pages is used, it is common for the experiment number to be the number of the page on which the experiment starts. The way in which the notebook is indexed is open to personal preference. In this system a researcher's first book is book *A*, then *B,C,D* etc. Figure 2.1 therefore shows experiment *23* of book *A*. Compounds isolated from this experiment all carry the number *A23*, prefixed with the researchers initials (in this case *BB*). When more than one product is isolated from a reaction a suffix, *a, b, c* etc. is added to the reference number, *a* being the spot running highest on tlc, *b* the next, and so on. Thus, for this experiment two products were isolated and these carry reference numbers *BB A23a* and *BB A23b*. Using this system the origin of any synthetic sample can be determined very quickly.

3. The date

It is important that the date is always included.

4. A reaction scheme indicating the proposed transformation

This is always included at the top of the page so that an individual experiment is easily found. If the reaction proceeded as desired the scheme is left intact, but if the desired product was not obtained it can be crossed through in red to indicate this. If other products were also obtained they can be added, again in a different colour ink if desired. Thus, simply flicking through the lab book, looking at the schemes, can quickly provide a good deal of information. Some people prefer to write only the left-hand side of the equation until the experiment is complete.

Ref., J.-L. Luche, L. Rodriguez-Hahn and P. Crabbe, J. Chem. Soc., Chem. Commun., 1978, 601

Substance	Quant.	Mol. wt.	m.moles	Equiv.	Source
BB A21a	200mg	348	0.57		p.A21
NaBH4	27mg	38	0.71	2.84	Aldrich
CeCl3(0.4M/MeOH)	2ml		0.8	1.4	
MeOH	25ml				

Method:
    The aldehyde (200mg) and CeCl3 solution 2ml) in MeOH (25ml), was cooled to $0^{o}C$, then treated with NaBH4 (27mg in MeOH, 8ml) .

TLC

10 min	30 min
4:1 Pet/EtOAc	4:1 Pet/EtOAc

←——BB A23a (red/brown - vanilin)

←——BB A23b (blue - vanilin)

SM   Rxn   SM   Rxn

After 30 min tlc shows no SM, but two products. MeOH was evaporated, CH2Cl2 (30ml) added and the mixture washed with 10% HCl (10ml) followed by satd. NaHCO3 (3 X10ml), dried and evaporated. (210mg crude)

Flash chromatography using 9:1 (pet. ether/EtOAc) on 8g of silica provided:

BB A23a 27mg (12%)- NMR (BB28), MS (BB19), IR (BB27) , Data sheet 6 - looks like:

$C_{25}H_{30}O_4$
mw = 394

BB A23b 140 mg (69% yield) - NMR (BB29), MS (BB20), IR (BB28) , Data sheet 5 - OK for:

$C_{23}H_{26}O_3$
mw = 350

Comment:
    Next time use aqueous solvent - may avoid ketal formation

Figure 2.1

5. *Literature references (if there are any)*

6. *Quantities*

The quantities of each ingredient of the reaction are listed at the beginning, together with the molecular weight, number of moles and number of molar equivalents. It is very useful to have this information available at a glance. Having the molecular weights on hand saves a good deal of time when going on to other reactions and when looking at mass spectra etc., but the real importance of this section is that the values contained here are critical when evaluating the outcome of a reaction, and you might want to adjust them in subsequent modifications of the procedure.

7. *The procedure*

This should be an exact account of the practical procedure carried out, including any spillages or other mishaps. It can be quite brief and not necessarily of publication standard, as long as it is understandable.

8. *Reaction monitoring*

Tlc is the most widely used method for reaction monitoring and it is very important to include a full size representation of the tlc plate(s) used, *giving the development solvent* and the stain used for visualization. Tlc gives us a true feel for the reaction and a good picture of a tlc is worth many words when it comes to following a procedure. In some cases hplc, gc, or other technique will be used to monitor the progression of the reaction and again a representation of this should be included. Some people find that it is more convenient to draw the tlcs on the adjacent notebook page. (For more details about tlc, see Chapter 8)

9. *Details of work-up and purification of the product(s)*

For chromatography it is important to include the quantity and type of adsorbent, and the solvent system used for elution. Some people also like to include a tlc representation of the column fractions. If the product is purified by crystallization, record the solvent used and the m.p. If it is distilled describe the type of distillation set-up and record the b.p. and pressure.

10. Cross references to the spectra and data book(sheet)

All compounds should be given reference numbers, as described above, and these should be cross referenced with data book entries and the reference numbers of the corresponding spectra. Indeed, many people like to use the same number for the spectra. The yield of each compound isolated should also be given and if possible its structure.

11. Finally include any concluding remarks about the reaction.

2.3   Keeping records of data

When it comes to writing reports, papers, and especially theses, one of the most time consuming and tedious jobs is collecting together experimental and spectroscopic data for compounds, and it can be very frustrating to find that a particular piece of data has been mislaid or was never obtained. Also, when the collecting of such data is left to the time of report writing, errors can easily creep into spectral assignments. It is a much better practice to collect data and make spectral assignments as your work progresses and keep this information stored in a standard format.

Whenever a significant compound has been synthesized a data sheet or data book page should be created for it. The format of a data sheet can vary according to personal preferences, but it should contain at least the following pieces of information:

1. The structure and molecular formula of the compound
2. A procedure for the preparation of the compound, preferably in a style suitable for publication.
3. An appropriate range of spectroscopic and chromatographic data which is sufficient to characterize the compound. *Full assignments of spectra should be entered in the data sheets as soon as the information is obtained, then when it comes to report writing most of the information required is on hand.*
4. Cross references to spectra and lab notebook
5. Literature references, if there are any

2.3.1   What types of data should be collected ?

There is now a plethora of spectroscopic and chromatographic techniques available for determining the structure and purity of organic compounds and it is therefore impossible to give a hard and fast rule stating the type of data which should be obtained on every compound. Because of the rapid expansion in the variety of techniques available there is presently much debate about what constitutes a rigorous structure and purity analysis. Traditionally, microanalysis was held to be the single standard test to which any new organic molecule was subjected, and in some instances you may find that it is a mandatory requirement. This is often the case for patent applications. However, many researchers now prefer to use a range of spectroscopic and chromatographic techniques to determine the structure and purity of their compounds, and each researcher or research group will be biased towards the particular types of data they find appropriate to characterize the type of compounds that they work with.

For each individual compound you should decide first of all how rigorously it needs to be characterized, then decide upon the appropriate techniques to do this. For known compounds structure proof is often trivial and simple techniques such as mixed melting point should not be overlooked. If you are working on a synthetic sequence where the structures of some of your intermediates are well established, it is not always necessary to treat each individual compound as a complete unknown. This is especially true if the reaction which has been carried out is a very simple one, such as the reduction of an aldehyde to a primary alcohol. On the other hand, when a crucial reaction has been carried out you should be very careful to choose a characterization technique which gives you the structural information you require, unambiguously.

2.3.2 Formats for data records

If you choose to keep a data book, it is a good idea to start each new entry on the next free right hand page of the book. The data for some compounds will not fill the space allocated, but it is best to allow a reasonable space, because some compounds will require a large amount of spectroscopic data for characterization.

Data sheets are an alternative to the data book. These can be of a standardized design with spaces for each type of data to be filled in. The advantage of this system is that it is easy to see at a glance whether a particular piece of data has been obtained for a compound. However, two disadvantages of the fixed format data sheet are: it does not provide the flexibility which is often required to record diverse types of data which may be used to characterize a particular compound; and it tends to encourage the mistaken idea that every compound requires the same characterization data. The system we prefer for data records, is one which makes use of a micro computer word processor. A standard format blank data sheet, as shown below, is kept on disk (Fig. 2.2).

DATA SHEET

Chemical Name:

Scheme:

Lit. Refs:

Method:

Mol. Formula:

m.p./b.p.:	$^{\circ}$C
Tlc :	R_f (pet. ether/ethyl acetate,)
$[\alpha]^D_{25}$:	$^{\circ}$ (c = , CHCl$_3$)
^1H *nmr (MHz):*	δ
^{13}C *nmr (MHz):*	δ
ν_{max}:	cm^{-1}
λ_{max}:	nm
m/z (NH$_4$, CI):	

Found M , calc. for

Analysis: Found C%; H%; N%; O%,

Calc. for CHNO = C%; H%; N%; O%

Notebook:

Spectra:

Figure 2.2

When a new compound is synthesized a blank data sheet is modified with the data of the compound and a data record is created which is tailored to the needs of the particular compound. Any of the data types which are inappropriate for characterization of a particular compound can be removed, and any additional data types can be added if required. This is especially

---

(±)-*Exo,exo*-7,8-Dibenzyloxy-*exo-cis*-bicyclo[3.3.0]-oct-2-en-4-ol-2-carboxaldehyde

Method:

To a stirred solution of oxalyl chloride (100ml, 1.10mmol) in dry dichloromethane (15ml) at -78°C, a solution of dimethylsulphoxide (200ml, 2.58mmol) in dichloromethane (1ml) was added dropwise. The reaction mixture was stirred for 5 min, then epoxide (200mg, 0.55mmol) in dichloromethane (2ml) was added dropwise. The resulting mixture was stirred for a further 20 min, then triethylamine (1ml, 7.61mmol) was added. After 10 min at -78°C the mixture was allowed to warm to room temperature, then poured into 2M HCl (30ml) and extracted with dichloromethane (2 x 30ml). The extract was washed with saturated aqueous $NaHCO_3$ (40ml), then dried, and the solvent removed *in vacuo*.

The crude product was taken up in dichloromethane (15ml), 1,5-diazabicyclo[5.4.0]undec-5-ene (167mg, 1.1 mmol) was added, and the mixture was stirred at room temperature for 2h. The solution was then poured into 2M HCl (20ml), extracted with dichloromethane (2 x 30ml), and washed with saturated aqueous $NaHCO_3$ (40ml), then dried, and the solvent removed *in vacuo*. Tlc. examination of the crude mixture showed the presence of one major product. An analytical sample of the hydroxy enal was obtained by flash chromatography (1:1 pet. ether/ethyl acetate), yield, 80%.

Mol. Formula:	$C_{23}H_{24}O_4$ (mw = 364)
Tlc:	R_f 0.23 (uv-active; pet. ether/ethyl acetate, 1:1)
ν_max.:	3600-3200, 3075, 3050, 2750,1690 and 700cm^{-1}
m/z (FAB+, thioglycerol):	365 (M + 1, 9.6%), 364 (M+), 92 and 57 (100%)
Notebook:	BB D45b
Spectra:	nmr 257; ms 163; ir 250

^{1}H nmr (300 MHz):

δ value	Proton(s)	Mult.	J value/Hz (coupled proton)
9.73	H-10	s	
7.5-7.15	Ar	m	
6.55	H-7	~t	J = 1.0 (H-6) and 1.0 (H-9)
4.70	PhC<u>H</u>2	m	
4.50	H-6	dd	J = 1.5 (H-5) and 1.0 (H-7)
4.30	PhC<u>H</u>2	m	
3.80	H-1	dd	J = 4.5 (H-3) and 1.0 (H-9)
3.58	H-9	ddd	J = 8.0 (H-5), 1.0 (H-7) and 1.0 (H-1)
3.47	H-3	ddd	J = 11.0 (H-4b), 6.5 (H-4a) and 4.5 (H-1)
2.68	H-5	m	J = 9.0 (H-4b), 8.0 (H-9), 1.5(H-4a) and 1.5 (H-6)
2.37	H-4b	ddd	J = 12.5 (H-4a), 11.0 (H-3) and 9.0 (H-5)
1.84	H-4a	ddd	J = 12.5 (H-4b), 6.5 (H-3) and 1.5 (H-5)
1.65	OH	bs	

Figure 2.3

useful for nmr data, which can be as simple as a list of 60MHz signals, or could comprize a vast array of information from a high field FT instrument such as, coupling constants, nOe's or 2D data. Once the data sheets have been printed out they are kept in a ring file, to make a very flexible data book. Similar non-computer based record systems can also be devised but the advantage of using a computer is that the record can easily be updated at any time. When designing our data sheet we decided upon a standard style which we also use for experimental sections of reports and theses. Therefore, if a researcher is conscientious about keeping data records up to date the tedium is taken out of reporting results. Also, with only slight modifications, the data record can become an experimental entry which fits the style of any major journal. An example of a completed data record is shown in Fig. 2.3. Notice that there are some quite detailed high field nmr data which are represented in a table. The table is also a standard design and provides a good way of presenting complex nmr data so that they can be deciphered quickly.

CHAPTER 3

Equipping the Laboratory and the Bench

3.1 Introduction

In this chapter we will describe general laboratory and bench equipment which we have found to be of great use when working with modern organic chemical reactions.

Many modern procedures which have now become standard methodology in organic chemistry require dry reaction conditions, and often an inert atmosphere. This has had a dramatic effect on the way efficient laboratory facilities are arranged. Not so long ago reactions involving anhydrous, inert conditions were rare and it was expedient to arrange the equipment for such procedures on a one-off basis. However, now that this type of reaction is common place, it makes sense to set up the laboratory in such a way that reactions under inert conditions can be carried out as a matter of routine. This chapter is written with this principle in mind. Much of the equipment introduced here will be discussed in more detail in subsequent chapters.

3.2 Setting up the laboratory

The basic furniture provided in organic chemistry laboratories will vary considerably from one establishment to another and clearly any advice given in this chapter will have to be tailored to the facilities available. The ideal layout of the lab is also a very subjective matter and the advice given here is therefore not intended to be taken as gospel, but simply reflects the experiences of the authors from various laboratories in which they have worked.

When setting up the lab it is usual for some areas of bench space to be set aside for communal apparatus, and other parts to be allocated as individual benches. Clearly, the areas which are assigned as communal bench space will depend on the amount and type of communal equipment which is to be installed. In this chapter some pieces of equipment will be identified as communal and others as part of the individual bench kit, but the classification will vary from one laboratory to another. The distinction will to some extent depend on the type of work being undertaken, but will also depend on the budget and space available.

Unless alternative office space is provided, it is a good idea to have some desk space in the lab where workers can read and write, away from areas used for chemicals. Desk space may also be required for small computers which are also becoming a common feature of the modern organic chemistry lab. Drawers or filing cabinets are useful for the safe storage of spectra and other paperwork, and a blackboard is an invaluable laboratory aid.

The area which constitutes an individual 'bench' will vary considerably from one lab to another. In our view all procedures involving organic chemicals should be carried out in an efficient fume cupboard. This implies that each full-time worker in an organic chemistry lab permanently requires *at least* one metre of fume cupboard space. However, in practice it is often the case, particularly in academic labs, that much less fume cupboard space is actually provided, and fume cupboards may be communal. In this chapter the term 'bench' will refer to the space occupied by an individual worker and it will be assumed that this space incorporates an adequate area of fume cupboard, **where all reactions are carried out.**

3.3 General laboratory equipment

In this section we describe the communal facilities that should be found in a laboratory in which modern organic chemistry is undertaken. Careful thought should go into the placing of communal equipment. It may be quite reasonable to place unattended items such as a fridge or oven in an awkward corner, but a piece of apparatus at which a person will be working should be in a position where the operator has enough room to work without hindering anybody else. Equipment such as stills, which are used regularly by all members of the lab, should be located so that they are easily accessible, without causing a disturbance to anyone working close by.

Rotary evaporators

Rotary evaporators are perhaps the most heavily used pieces of equipment in an organic research lab. They should therefore be located conveniently throughout the lab, or preferably, each worker should have his or her own on the bench.

Fridge and/or freezer

A fridge and/or freezer should be provided to store chemicals, and this should never be used for food storage.

Glass drying oven(s)

Again these should be conveniently located.

Vacuum oven

This may be used infrequently, but is still a very valuable piece of equipment.

Balances

A two place balance is indispensable and a four place balance needs to be available for small scale work. When locating these remember that they are used frequently, by people carrying out careful work, so do not put them in the way of others, also avoid drafts and vibrations.

Kugelrohr bulb to bulb distillation apparatus (e.g. Buchi)

This apparatus is invaluable when preparing relatively small quantities of high-boiling liquids. It is relatively mobile and can be moved from bench to bench and attached to various vacuum sources. However, it is useful to locate it near to a high vacuum pump, where it is normally used.

Vacuum pumps

Vacuum at various levels will be required around the lab. Each bench should have a modest vacuum source available (about 20mmHg), and this can be provided by a water aspirator, a house vacuum system or a small diaphragm pump. This level of vacuum is sufficient for rotary evaporation of most solvents, filtering under vacuum, distillation of relatively volatile oils, and similar tasks. However, there are a variety of operations for which a high vacuum pump is either preferable or necessary. These operations include, removing last traces of solvent from small quantities of product, distillation of high-boiling oils and providing vacuum for a double manifold (described later). For most purposes a simple two stage rotary pump, which will provide a vacuum of <1mm, is adequate. If sufficient resources are available each bench should have a high vacuum pump, connected to a double manifold, but in many labs vacuum pumps are considered to be communal equipment. Whether or not pumps are used communally, it is a good idea to reserve one pump for distillations, so that a reliable high vacuum can always be obtained. This pump should be fitted with an efficient trapping system (see Chapter 7) to avoid solvent contamination, and can be either on a mobile trolley or in a fixed position, depending on the bench and floor space available. A pump which is used for distillations only does not require a manifold to be attached. It is useful to have a general purpose communal pump, attached to a single manifold (Fig. 3.1), which can be used for removing trace amounts of solvent, and for distillations.

connected to
→ high vacuum
pump *via* traps

connected to
vacuum gauge

high vacuum
stopcock

Figure 3.1

Inert gases

A constant supply of dry inert gas (usually argon or nitrogen) is now essential in an organic chemistry lab. Some labs will have nitrogen or argon on tap and this is ideal, provided there are enough outlets and the gas is dry. However, in most labs gas is supplied from cylinders, which take up a lot of space and are quite expensive to rent. It causes great inefficiency in a modern lab if there are too few inert gas outlets, and it is therefore important when setting up the lab to decide how many gas outlets are required. We suggest that there should be at least one outlet for each person working in the lab, plus one for each piece of apparatus (such as a still) which is kept permanently under inert gas. This may suggest that the same number of cylinders is required, but the cost of this is usually prohibitive and space can also be a problem. One efficient way to use cylinders to service a large number of permanent inert gas lines, is to fit them with multi-way needle valves (e.g. 3-way). These are available from gas line hardware suppliers at a very modest cost and give several gas outlets for the price of one!

Having decided on the number of gas cylinders required these should be positioned in the laboratory so that semi-permanent PVC (Tygon) tubing lines can easily be taken to each bench and to each piece of apparatus requiring a supply. Some of the apparatus commonly used in conjunction with inert gases will be described below and in Chapters 6 and 8.

Solvent stills

Two basic types of solvent still are found in the lab, one is for distillation of solvents for routine use and the other is for distillation of ultra-dry solvents for carrying out reactions under dry conditions. Unless very high grade solvents are purchased, most solvents used in the lab for reactions or chromatography should be distilled. For solvents which are used regularly it is best to set up permanent stills and some typical designs for these are given in Chapter 4. Routine stills are usually quite large (up to 5 litres), and so therefore take several bottles of solvent at a time. Permanent large scale stills should normally be available for petroleum ether (usually the largest still), ethyl acetate, methylene chloride and any other solvents, according to your particular needs.

Some solvents, such as tetrahydrofuran and diethyl ether (there may be others you require also) are frequently required in very dry form, and it is inconvenient to set up a still each time a small quantity is required for a trial reaction. The efficiency of an organic lab is therefore greatly enhanced by having these dry solvents available 'on-tap' from permanent stills, which provide very effective drying, and are kept under an inert atmosphere. Modern designs for permanent stills used for these distillations are very compact, and do not cause inconvenience (see Chapter 4). A permanent still should be installed for any solvent which is used regularly in the lab. It is also worth keeping a spare distillation apparatus on hand for occasions when a less common dry solvent is required.

General distillation equipment

Apart from standard Quickfit equipment, labs should also have some one-piece distillation kits, which provide more effective distillation. A short-path distillation apparatus is very useful for low-holdup, high-throughput distillations, particularly on a small scale. These can be made by a glassblower, and one design is shown in Fig. 3.2.

	A	B	C	D	E	F
Size 1	5.5cm	3.5cm	6cm	2cm	B14	B14
Size 2	11cm	3.5cm	13cm	3cm	B24	B14

Figure 3.2

For fractional distillation a one-piece apparatus incorporating small fractionating columns is useful, and again two sizes are frequently used (Fig. 3.3; see also Chapters 5 and 9).

General laboratory glassware

In any lab there will be quite a number of pieces of glassware which it is only practical to keep communally, this is especially true for large equipment. However, the nature of this equipment will vary a good deal, depending on the type of work being undertaken.

	A	B	C
Size1	8cm	3.5cm	13cm
Size 2	18cm	3.5cm	18cm

Figure 3.3

Chromatographic equipment

Tlc is by far the most widely used technique for rapid, routine reaction monitoring and it is essential that the lab should have permanent facilities for visualization of tlc plates. A range of solvent dips, an iodine tank and a small uv lamp are usually all that is necessary (see Chapter 8).

More sophisticated chromatographic techniques are also finding much wider application in organic chemistry labs, and both hplc and capillary gc instruments are now quite common-place. These techniques complement tlc as analytical techniques and, although an initial investment of time is necessary to learn how to use the instrumentation, this pays good dividends in the long run (see Chapters 8 and 9).

3.4   The individual bench

There are a variety of factors that influence the proportion of laboratory equipment which is part of an individual bench set, and that which is communal. In most academic research labs workers find it most convenient to keep a more or less complete set of routine glassware as part of the bench kit. The individual then looks after the set, replaces broken equipment, and keeps it clean, so that any particular piece of equipment is available when required. On the other hand, in an industrial lab there is normally an extensive range of communal routine glassware which is washed by lab helpers, and there is little need for workers to keep a full set of bench equipment. In either type of situation there are certain pieces of equipment which individuals usually like to keep for personal use, including such things as syringes and chromatography columns. Whether more specialized or sophisticated equipment is communal or personal will depend, to some extent, on how frequently it is used, and on the funds available. A list of equipment which we find useful to keep as part of the bench set is given below, with a brief description of some of the more specialized items.

3.4.1 Routine glassware

A typical bench set of routine glassware, excluding specialized equipment, is given below.

Item	Quantity
Adapter reduction B14 socket B24 cone	1
Adapter reduction B10 socket B14 cone	1
Adapter tube B14 cone	1
Adapter expansion B24 socket B14 cone	1
Adapter expansion B29 socket B24 cone	1
Beakers low form 10ml	2
Beakers low form 25ml	4
Beakers low form 100ml	4
Beakers low form 400ml	2
Cylinders measuring 10ml	1
Cylinders measuring 25ml	1
Cylinders measuring 100ml	1

Cylinders measuring (stoppered) 1000ml	1
Funnels filter 15.00cm	1
Funnels filter 7.5cm	1
Funnels separating 250ml	1
Funnels separating 50ml	1
Funnels separating 1000ml	1
Flask conical 100ml	4
Flask conical 250ml	2
Flask conical 500ml	2
Flask round-bottom 10ml B14 socket	6
Flask round-bottom 50ml B14 socket	6
Flask round-bottom 100ml B24 socket	6
Flask round-bottom 250ml B24 socket	3
Flask round-bottom 500ml B24 socket	2
Flask round bottom 1000ml B24 socket	1

3.4.2 Personal items

There are certain items which individuals usually prefer to keep for their own personal use, even when routine glassware is communal. Here is a list of standard, commercially-available items which we think should be kept as the bench kit:

Item	Quantity
Spatulas (various sizes)	-
Magnetic followers 25.00mm	4
Magnetic followers 12.5mm	4
Magnetic followers 25.00mm (oval)	1
Magnetic followers 50.00mm (oval)	1
Syringe needles 6 inch S-S Luer fit	6
Syringe needles 12 inch S-S Luer fit	6
Syringe with metal Luer lock 2ml	2
Syringe with metal Luer lock 5ml	2
Syringe with metal Luer lock 10ml	2
Luer lock tubing adapter	1
Thermometers -10 to 360°C	1
Thermometers -10 to 110°C	1
Thermometers -100 to 10°C	1
Thermometers, quickfit B14 -10 to 360°C	1
Pasteur pipettes	1 box
Vials (1 & 5 dram)	1 box

3.4.3 Specialized personal items

There are some specialized pieces of glassware which we find to be extremely useful to have as part of the bench set and these will be briefly described here, but for full details of how they are used see the appropriate chapter.

The double manifold

Figure 3.4

If you would like to carry out reactions under dry and/or inert conditions as a matter of routine, the double manifold is perhaps the single most useful item of equipment which will enable you to do this. We recommend that this be a standard item of equipment, permanently fitted to every individual bench and connected to the laboratory inert gas supply by PVC (Tygon) tubing. The manifold consists of two glass barrels, one evacuated and one filled with an inert gas. An outlet is supplied by either barrel of the manifold *via* a two-way double oblique tap (see Figs. 3.4 and 3.5). Thus, at the turn of the tap, equipment connected to the manifold can be alternately evacuated or filled with inert gas.

Figure 3.5 Cross section through a double oblique tap

A bubbler should be incorporated in the line from the cylinder which feeds the inert gas barrel and it should have a built in anti suck-back valve to avoid oil contaminating the manifold (Fig. 3.6).

Figure 3.6

A rotary pump is normally connected to the vacuum barrel of the manifold and a schematic diagram showing the complete set-up is shown in Fig. 3.7.

Figure 3.7

Although it is preferable for workers to have their own individual manifold, in some labs this may not be possible, because of insufficient fume cupboard space or lack of pumps. In this case, manifolds can be treated as communal items of equipment, but discipline must be observed to keep the manifold clean and avoid cross-contamination.

Another type of manifold which is useful for carrying out reactions under inert atmosphere is the 'spaghetti tubing' manifold (Fig. 3.8). This is a single barrel inert gas manifold, fitted with narrow bore Teflon tubing outlets. Each outlet has a syringe needle attached which can be pushed through a septum to provide an inert atmosphere within a flask. This type of system is particularly useful for small scale work.

Figure 3.8

Full descriptions of how to use manifolds are given in Chapters 5 and 8.

Three-way Quickfit gas inlet T taps

A simple piece of equipment which is applicable to a variety of tasks is a 3-way teflon tap connected to a Quickfit cone joint (Fig. 3.9).

Figure 3.9

These are so universally useful that we suggest you have at least three of the B14 size and two of the B24 size as part of your personal bench set. They are particularly useful when used in conjunction with a double manifold. With the inert gas from the manifold connected to the horizontal inlet and the tap in position A (Fig. 3.10), a reaction flask can be kept under a slight positive inert gas pressure. If the gas flow is increased and the tap is turned to position B, liquids can be introduced *via* the vertical inlet, whilst maintaining an inert atmosphere (see Chapters 5 and 8 for more details).

Another simple use is for connecting flasks to a high vacuum system for removal of last traces of solvent.

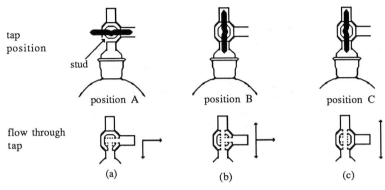

Figure 3.10

Filtering aids

Rapid filtration is often needed, and the speed of filtration is increased dramatically by applying pressure or a vacuum. There are two types of one-piece sintered funnels which we find very useful, as shown in Fig. 3.11. The parallel-sided type are constructed by fusing a circular sinter into the appropriate diameter glass tubing, which is then joined to a cone joint and a piece of narrow-bore tubing (about 10mm od). It is useful to have two or three of these in the bench kit, ranging in diameters of between 1 and 10cm. The larger ones are particularly valuable for filtering off drying agent, leaving the the dried solution in a round-bottom flask, from which solvent can be evaporated directly. One or two of the smaller Hirsch-style funnels are useful and these are more commonly used for filtering off crystals after small-scale recrystallizations, the mother liquor being conveniently deposited in a round-bottom flask. These can be made starting from a sintered funnel, but a glassblower can make them more cheaply by inserting a circular sinter into a narrow tube, then forming the funnel from this.

Two other pieces of equipment of value as filtration aids are the Craig tube (Fig. 3.12a, see Chapter 9), used for very small recrystallizations, and a sintered funnel (Fig. 3.12b) for filtration under inert atmosphere (see Chapter 5 for more details).

	A	B
size 1	5cm	4cm
size 2	7.5cm	4cm

	C	D	E
size 1	5cm	5cm	5.5cm
size 2	7.5cm	7cm	5.5cm
size 3	10cm	9cm	5.5cm

Figure 3.11

(a) Craig tube

(b) inert atmosphere filter

Figure 3.12

Glassware for chromatography

Flash chromatography (see Chapter 9) is probably the most effective method available for rapid routine purification and separation of reaction products. To gain expertise in flash chromatography it is a sound idea to have a familiar set of columns on hand, and it is useful to have a set of about five, ranging in diameter from about 5mm to 50mm, as part of the bench kit (Fig. 3.13b). A convenient length for all columns is 25cm, except for those with a very narrow bore, which can be shorter. Reservoirs will also be required for flash chromatography, 250ml, 500ml, and 1 litre being useful sizes (Fig. 3.13c). Another useful item is a simple 'flash valve' (Fig. 3.13a) that will limit the pressure applied to the column, thus making the operation safer by reducing the possibility of column fracture. All this equipment is described in more detail in Chapter 9.

(a) flash valve   (b) flash column   (c) reservoir

Figure 3.13

CHAPTER 4

Purification and Drying of Solvents

4.1 Introduction

The use of appropriately purified solvents is vital to the success of the procedures for which they are used. It is important to note that the degree of purity and dryness required depends on the intended application, so when choosing a method from this chapter remember to pick one which is appropriate for your purpose. Consult Appendix 1 for useful data about commonly used organic solvents.

Remember that solvents are hazardous materials and beware particularly of the flammability of the hydrocarbons and ether, the toxicity of benzene, chloroform, and carbon tetrachloride, and the possibility of peroxide contamination of ethereal solvents.

4.2 Purification of solvents

The most commonly used grade of solvent is 'reagent grade' which typically means 97-99% purity with small amounts of water and other volatile impurities as listed in the specification. This is adequate for use in extractions and in many chemical reactions. However, some applications are more demanding and require either the use of commercial solvents of higher purity, or the purification of commercially available products. Notable examples include the following.

1. Reactions involving strongly basic organometallic compounds, e.g. Grignard reagents, organolithiums, and metal hydrides, require the use of carefully dried solvents. Anhydrous solvents (< 50ppm of water)

are available but they are more expensive and less reliable than solvents dried by the techniques described below.

2. Solvents used for spectroscopy, especially nmr and uv, should be of high purity. Many suppliers provide 'spectroscopic grade' solvents which are particularly suitable for uv spectroscopy because ultraviolet absorbing impurities have been removed.

3. Solvents used for chromatography should always be fractionally distilled to ensure that non-volatile impurities are removed. Solvents for hplc should be of high purity and again many suppliers provide special 'hplc grade' solvents, which have been purified and filtered to remove contaminants which might degrade hplc columns.

4. All applications involving quantitative analysis require the use of 'analytical grade' (typically >99.5% purity) solvents. It is good practice in general to use high quality solvents for the purification of your products, and it is particularly important to use pure solvents when purifying samples for microanalysis.

In most cases purification of a solvent simply involves drying and distilling it, so the next sections are devoted to drying agents and methods used for drying common solvents, and the final section contains descriptions of typical continuous stills. Apart from water the only other commonly encountered contaminant is peroxidic material formed by aerial oxidation of ethereal solvents. Methods for dealing with these dangerous impurities are described in the section on the purification of diethyl ether.

4.3   Drying agents

Drying agents fall into two broad categories, those used for preliminary drying and the drying of extracts, and those used for rigorous drying. The pre-drying agents are largely interchangeable with each other and the choice is usually limited only by the chemical reactivity of some of the reagents. Preliminary drying of solvents, prior to rigorous drying, is essential unless the solvent already has a low (< 0.1%) water content. Of necessity the reagents used for thorough drying are very reactive and they must be treated with great care. In particular, it is important to make the right choice of drying agent for the solvent in question, in order to avoid dangerous or undesirable reactions between the solvent and the drying agent, and care must be taken to ensure the safe destruction and disposal of excess reagent remaining in solvent residues.

When the solvent is to be distilled after standing over a desiccant, the drying agent should be filtered off before distillation if it removes water reversibly, e.g. by hydrate formation ($MgSO_4$, $CaCl_2$), or by absorption (molecular sieves). The solvent can be distilled without removal of the desiccant in cases where water removal is irreversible (CaH_2, P_2O_5).

The recommendations in this and the following section are largely based on the work of Burfield and Smithers et al. who have carried out quantitative studies on the efficiency of drying agents for a wide range of solvents.[1] Their work has supplanted earlier studies many of which are of doubtful reliability. Other useful sources of information include Perrin and Armarego[2], and Riddick, Bunger, and Sakano.[3]

Alumina, Al$_2$O$_3$

Neutral or basic alumina of activity grade I is an efficient drying agent for hydrocarbons, 5% w/v loading giving extremely dry solvents. It is also useful for the purification of chloroform.

Barium oxide, BaO

The commercially available anhydrous product is an inexpensive drying agent which is useful for amines and pyridines (30-50ppm after standing for 24h over 5% w/v). It is strongly basic and is ineffective for alcohols and dipolar aprotic solvents.

Boric anhydride, B$_2$O$_3$

Recommended drying agent for acetone, and effective also for thorough drying of acetonitrile.

1. (a) D.R. Burfield, K.H. Lee, and R.H. Smithers, *J. Org. Chem.*, 1977, **42**, 3060; (b) D.R. Burfield, G.H. Gan, and R.H. Smithers, *J. Appl. Chem. Biotechnol.*, 1978, **28**, 23; (c) D.R. Burfield and R.H. Smithers, *J. Org. Chem.*, 1978, **43**, 3966; (d) D.R. Burfield and R.H. Smithers, *J. Chem. Technol. Biotechnol.*, 1980, **30**, 491; (e) D.R. Burfield and R.H. Smithers, and A.S.C. Tan, *J. Org. Chem.*, 1981, **46**, 629; (f) D.R. Burfield and R.H. Smithers, *J. Chem. Educ.*, 1982, **59**, 703; (g) D.R. Burfield and R.H. Smithers, *J. Org. Chem.*, 1983, **48**, 2420.
2. D.D. Perrin and W.L.F. Armarego, *Purification of Laboratory Chemicals*, 3rd ed., Pergamon, Oxford, 1988.
3. J.A. Riddick, W.B. Bunger, and T.K. Sakano, *Organic Solvents, Physical Properties and Methods of Purification*, 4th ed., Wiley-Interscience, New York, 1986.

Calcium chloride, CaCl₂

Both the powder and pellet forms are effective for pre-drying hydrocarbons and ethers. It reacts with acids, alcohols, amines, and some carbonyl compounds.

Calcium hydride, CaH₂

The reagent of choice for rigorous drying amines, pyridines, and HMPA, and effective also for hydrocarbons, alcohols, ethers, and DMF. It is available in powdered or granular form, the granular is preferable if it is to be stored for any length of time. The granules should be crushed immediately before use and residues should be destroyed by *careful* addition of water (H_2 evolution).

Calcium sulphate, CaSO₄

Available as 'Drierite', it is only suitable for drying organic extracts. The blue self-indicating version should not be used to dry liquids because the coloured compound may leach into the solvent.

Lithium aluminium hydride, LiAlH₄

Although widely used for drying ethers, it is less effective than other methods and is extremely dangerous.
Its use is strongly discouraged.

Magnesium, Mg

Recommended for methanol and ethanol.

Magnesium sulphate, MgSO₄

The monohydrate is fast acting and has a high capacity (forms a heptahydrate), making it the desiccant of choice for organic extracts. It is slightly acidic so care is required with very sensitive compounds. It is not efficient enough to be useful for pre-drying.

Molecular sieves

These are sodium and calcium aluminosilicates which have cage-like crystal lattice structures containing pores of various sizes, depending on their constitution. They can absorb small molecules, such as water, which can fit into the pores. The most commonly used types 3A, 4A, and 5A have pore sizes of approximately 3Å, 4Å, and 5Å respectively, and they are available in bead or powder form. After activation at 250-320°C for a minimum of 3h they are probably the most powerful desiccants available[1(b)]. They can be stored in a desiccator or in an oven at >100°C for a few weeks but they are rapidly hydrated in the air. If you are doubtful about the effectiveness of an old batch, place a few beads in the palm of your hand and add a drop of water - if the sieves are active you should feel a distinctly exothermic reaction. In most cases extremely dry solvent can be obtained simply by batchwise drying over sieves, i.e. allowing the solvent to stand over 5% w/v of sieves for 12h, decanting, adding a second batch of sieves etc. Sieves absorb water reversibly so a solvent should always be decanted from the sieves prior to distillation. 4A Beads are recommended for thorough drying of amines, DMF, DMSO, and HMPA, and almost all rigorously dried solvents are best stored over 5% w/v of 4A sieves. However, only the 3A form is suitable for drying acetonitrile, methanol, and ethanol, and higher alcohols require the use of powdered 3A sieves. They are not useful for drying acetone because they cause self-condensation. Provided that they are not discoloured, sieves can be reused by washing well with a volatile organic solvent, allowing to dry, drying at 100°C for several hours, and then reactivating at 300°C.

Phosphorus pentoxide, P_2O_5

(Causes burns)   Although a rapid and efficient desiccant its use is limited by its high chemical reactivity. It reacts with alcohols, amines, acids, and carbonyl compounds and causes significant decomposition of HMPA, DMSO, and acetone. It is useful for drying acetonitrile and may be used for hydrocarbons and ethers but is less convenient than other reagents. It is often used in desiccators. It is best decomposed by careful portionwise addition to ice-water followed by neutralization with base (do not add water to P_2O_5, the mixture may become so hot that the vessel could crack). It is extremely efficient for drying gases and is available in a convenient form, mixed with an inert support, so that it does not become syrupy.

Potassium hydroxide, KOH

(Causes burns)   Freshly powdered KOH is a good drying agent for amines and pyridines but is inferior to calcium hydride. It should not be used with base sensitive solvents.

Sodium, Na

Sodium is widely used to dry hydrocarbons and ethers. It may be formed into wire using a sodium press or used as granules by cutting the bars under petroleum ether. It suffers from the disadvantage that the metal surface rapidly becomes coated with an inert material so it should not be used unless the solvent is pre-dried. Sodium reacts with benzophenone to give a dark blue ketyl radical which is protonated by water to give colourless products. Thus the sodium-benzophenone system is particularly convenient because it is self-indicating, and it is the preferred reagent for rigorous drying of ether, THF, DME, and other ethereal solvents. Sodium-potassium alloy has been recommended because it is liquid and therefore its surface does not become coated so easily, but this advantage is outweighed by the increased danger resulting from the use of potassium. Sodium residues can be destroyed by slow careful addition of ethanol until hydrogen evolution ceases. The mixture should then be stirred well, to ensure that no coated lumps of sodium remain, before carefully adding methanol. After leaving for several hours the mixture should be stirred again to ensure that all of the sodium has been consumed, and then the mixture should be added cautiously to a large excess of water before disposal.

Sodium should never be added to chlorinated solvents because a vigorous or explosive reaction could occur.

Sodium sulphate, Na_2SO_4

Anhydrous sodium sulphate is a weak drying agent suitable only for drying extracts. It is preferable to magnesium sulphate for drying very acid sensitive compounds.

4.4   Drying of solvents

Solvents may be dried in individual batches using conventional distillation apparatus (Chapter 9), but it is more convenient to dry common solvents such as dichloromethane, ether, and THF in continuous stills (Section 4.5). In either case the solvent must be protected from moisture using an inert atmosphere (nitrogen or argon). Rigorously dried solvents must be stored under an inert atmosphere and handled using syringe or cannula techniques (Chapter 5).

Acetone

Acetone is completely miscible with water and its susceptibility to acid and base catalysed self condensation makes it particularly difficult to dry. Good results are obtained by drying over 3A sieves (10% w/v) overnight (any longer causes significant condensation), stirring over boric anhydride (5% w/v) for 24h, and then distilling[1(c)]. Distillation after 24h over boric anhydride or 6h over 3A sieves provides material which is adequate for most purposes.

Acetic acid

(Causes burns) Acetic acid is very hygroscopic. It can be dried by adding acetic anhydride (3% w/v) and distilling (b.p. 118°C). Reagent grade acetic acid usually contains some acetaldehyde. If this is likely to cause problems add chromium trioxide (2% w/v) as well as acetic anhydride before distilling, or use analytical grade material.

Acetonitrile

(Toxic) Preliminary drying is accomplished by stirring over potassium carbonate for 24h. A further 24h over 3A sieve or boric anhydride gives moderately dry solvent (~ 50ppm) but much better results are obtained by stirring over phosphorus pentoxide (5% w/v) for 24h. and then distilling[1(a)]. Drawbacks of this method are the formation of substantial quantities of coloured residue, and the possibility that the product is contaminated with traces of acidic impurities. If the acetonitrile is required for use with very acid sensitive compounds it is best to redistil it from potassium carbonate.

Ammonia

Distil from the cylinder into a flask cooled to <-40°C and fitted with a dry-ice condenser (Chapter 14). Add pieces of sodium until the dark blue colour persists, and then distil the ammonia into your reaction vessel.

Benzene

(Carcinogenic) Benzene, like most hydrocarbons is very easy to dry. No preliminary drying is required and several reagents will reduce the water content to < 1ppm. Alumina, calcium hydride, and 4A sieves (all 3% w/v for 6h) are the most convenient drying agents and the benzene is then distilled and stored over 4A sieves[1(a)]. Alternatively benzene may be dried over calcium hydride in a continuous still. Toluene may be dried in the same way.

tert-Butanol

Reflux over calcium hydride (5% w/v) and distil onto powdered 3A sieves[1(g)]. Other low molecular weight alcohols, but not methanol, can be dried in this way.

Carbon disulphide

(Highly flammable, toxic)   Distil (using a water bath) from calcium chloride or phosphorus pentoxide (2% w/v). *Do not use sodium or potassium.*

Carbon tetrachloride

(Carcinogenic)   See chloroform.

Chlorobenzene

See dichloromethane

Chloroform

(Toxic)   Perhaps the simplest procedure is to pass the chloroform through a column of basic alumina (grade I, 10g per 14ml). This removes traces of water and acid and also removes the ethanol which is present as a stabiliser. Carbon tetrachloride may be purified in the same way. Larger volumes of either solvent can be dried with 4A sieves, or by distillation from phosphorus pentoxide (3% w/v). Distilled chloroform should be stored in the dark to prevent formation of phosgene.

   Addition of sodium to chloroform or carbon tetrachloride may cause an explosion. Chloroform may also react explosively with strong bases and with acetone.

Cyclohexane

See petroleum ether.

Decalin (decahydronaphthalene)

Decalin is very easy to dry but it forms peroxides on prolonged contact with air so it is advisable to use a drying agent which will reduce the peroxides. Reflux over sodium for 2h and distil onto 4A sieves. Tetralin should be treated similarly.

1,2-Dichloroethane

See dichloromethane.

Dichloromethane

Reflux over calcium hydride (5% w/v) and distil onto 4A molecular sieves. Chlorobenzene and 1,2-dichloroethane can be dried in the same way. Dichloromethane can be dried over calcium hydride in a continuous still.

Never add sodium or powerful bases to chlorinated solvents - an explosion may occur. Reaction of azide salts with dichloromethane results in the formation of explosive azides.

Diethyl ether (ether)

(Flammable)   Ether itself, along with the other commonly used ethereal solvents, THF, DME, and dioxan, can contain substantial amounts of peroxides formed by exposure to the air. *These peroxides can cause serious explosions.* Test for the presence of peroxides by adding 1ml of the solvent to 1ml of a 10% solution of sodium iodide in acetic acid. A yellow colour indicates the presence of low concentrations of peroxides whereas a brown colour indicates high concentrations. Low concentrations of peroxides must be removed before further purification and a number of methods have been suggested[4]. One frequently recommended procedure is to shake the solvent with concentrated aqueous ferrous sulphate. Ethers are usually pre-dried over calcium chloride or sodium wire, and rigorously dried over sodium-benzophenone. Careful preliminary drying is necessary because all of these solvents can dissolve substantial quantities of water. The pre-dried solvent is then placed in a reflux apparatus or a continuous still and sodium pieces (1% w/v) and benzophenone (0.2% w/v) are added. The mixture is refluxed under an inert atmosphere until the deep blue colour of the ketyl radical anion persists. The ether may then be collected or distilled onto 4A sieves. This drying method also removes the peroxides which are a serious hazard when handling ethereal solvents. If a continuous still is used it will be necessary to add more sodium and benzophenone occasionally. Eventually the still will become very murky as the benzophenone reduction products accumulate. If this happens, or if the blue colour no longer persists, it is time to distil most of the solvent - do not distil to dryness. The sodium residues may then be destroyed as described in

4.   D.R. Burfield, *J. Org. Chem.*, 1982, **47**, 3821.

Section 4.3. Purified ethers are very susceptible to peroxide formation, so they should be stored in dark bottles under an inert atmosphere, and they should not be kept for more than a few weeks.

1,2-Dimethoxyethane (DME)

See diethyl ether.

Dimethylformamide (DMF)

Stir over calcium hydride or phosphorus pentoxide (5% w/v, overnight), filter, and distil (56°C at 20mmHg) onto 3A sieves[1(c)]. If phosphorus pentoxide is used a second distillation from potassium carbonate may be necessary. Alternatively, sequentially dry over three batches of 3A sieves (5% w/v, 12h).

Dimethyl sulphoxide (DMSO)

Distil (75°C at 12mmHg) discarding the first 20% and sequentially dry with two batches of 4A sieves (5% w/v, 12h)[1(c)]. Store over 4A sieves.

Dioxan

See diethyl ether.

Ethanol

Distil absolute alcohol from magnesium (as described for methanol) onto 3A molecular sieve powder or sequentially dry over two batches of 3A sieve powder (5% w/v, 12h)[1(g)].

Ether

See diethyl ether.

Ethyl acetate

Distil from potassium carbonate onto 4A sieves.

Hexamethylphosphoric triamide (HMPA)

(Carcinogenic) HMPA is very difficult to dry and even when stored over 4A sieves it needs to be dried afresh within a couple of weeks. Dry HMPA can be obtained by distilling (89°C at 3mmHg) from calcium hydride (10% w/v) onto 4A molecular sieve (20% w/v)[1(c)].

Hexane

See petroleum ether.

Methanol

(Toxic)   To dry 1 litre of methanol place magnesium turnings (5g) and iodine (0.5g) in a 2 litre flask fitted with a reflux condenser and add methanol (50ml). Warm the mixture until the iodine disappears, and if a stream of bubbles (hydrogen) is not observed add more iodine (0.5g). Continue heating until all of the magnesium has been consumed and then add the remainder of the methanol. Reflux the mixture for 3h , distil (bumping) onto 3A sieve beads (10% w/v), and allow to stand for at least 24h[1(g)].

Nitromethane

Dry by standing over calcium chloride, filtering, and distilling onto molecular sieves. Do not use phosphorus pentoxide.

Pentane

See petroleum ether.

Petroleum ether (petrol)

(Flammable)   This confusing name is used for mixtures of aliphatic hydrocarbons containing smaller amounts of aromatic compounds. It is generally supplied as several fractions each having a 20°C boiling range (40-60, 60-80 etc.). Alkane mixtures which do not contain aromatic compounds are supplied as pentane, hexane, cyclohexane etc. All of these solvents are readily dried by distilling, and standing over activity grade I alumina (5% w/v), or over 4A molecular sieves.

Pyridines

(Toxic)   Distil from calcium hydride onto 4A molecular sieves[1(e)].

Tetrahydrofuran (THF)

See diethyl ether.

Tetralin (tetrahydronaphthalene)

See decalin.

Toluene

See benzene.

Xylene

See benzene.

4.5 Solvent stills

There are two main types of solvent still that are commonly employed in organic research laboratories. One is the classical distillation set-up consisting of distillation pot, still-head, thermometer, condenser, receiver-adapter, and collection vessel. This arrangement is described in more detail

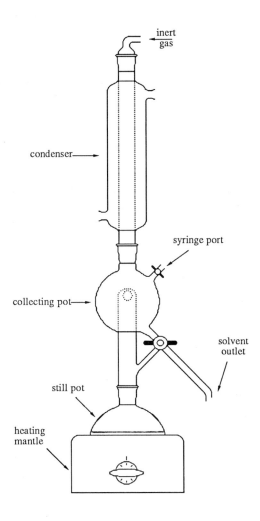

Figure 4.1

in Chapter 9, and is used for the distillation of solvents that are either required infrequently, or that can be stored without deterioration for long periods of time. The other is a continuous still set-up that consists of a distillation pot, collecting head, and condenser (see Fig. 4.1).

This type of still arrangement is used for solvents that are required on a regular basis and the still system is usually left set up, although generally it is only turned on when the solvent is required - *it is not recommended that any type of solvent still is left on unattended for prolonged periods of time* .

Continuous still systems typically have an upright arrangement that takes up less space than the conventional still set-up and a collecting vessel that is positioned between the still-pot and the condenser. The apparatus is designed such that the distilling solvent is condensed and collects in a collecting head. Once the collecting head is full the solvent simply overflows back into the still pot, allowing continuous distillation without the still boiling dry. The solvent can simply be drawn off from the collecting head when required, or poured back into the still pot if not.

Figure 4.2

A typical design for the continuous still collecting head is outlined in Fig. 4.2, and can be simply constructed from a round-bottom flask, ground glass cone, 2-way tap, and 3-way tap. The 2-way tap allows the solvent to be withdrawn *via* syringe which is particularly convenient for anhydrous solvents. The 3-way tap allows the solvent to be collected, drawn off, or poured back into the distillation pot. Obviously the size of the still depends upon the quantity of solvent required, however the still head should always be smaller in capacity than the still pot, so as to avoid the possibility of the still boiling dry.

When setting up a continuous still it is necessary to ensure that the solvent condenser is efficient, usually a double walled condenser is required (see Chapter 9), this is especially true for the lower boiling solvents. Also, all ground glass joints should be fitted with teflon sleeves to ensure a good seal, and prevent jamming. It is inadvisable to use grease on the joints since this will be leached out by the hot solvent, contaminating the solvent and causing the joints to stick. Similarly teflon taps are to be preferred over glass taps in the collecting head.

If an inert atmosphere is required for the solvent distillation, as is often the case for anhydrous solvents, then the continuous still system requires to be connected to a nitrogen or argon line (see Chapter 8). It is important when using such lines, you ensure that oil bubblers or similar devices do not suck back when the still is cooling. This often happens as a result of the gas volume of the still contracting as it cools, which creates a partial vacuum in the system. It is simply remedied by turning up the flow rate of the inert gas for the period whilst the still is cooling. It is also important that you do not heat up the still system without some mechanism for allowing the increase in gas volume to be released otherwise an explosion may result; this is prevented by incorporating an oil bubbler in the gas line (see Chapter 8).

The design of collecting heads can vary, for instance they can also be constructed using a conical flask instead of the round-bottom flask (Fig. 4.3a). Also, a more complex arrangement (Fig. 4.3b) incorporating a condenser to cool the distillate (particularly useful for high boiling solvents) is often used. This system also has the advantage of less ground glass joints in the set-up, although this can make cleaning the still head more difficult.

Purification and Drying of Solvents

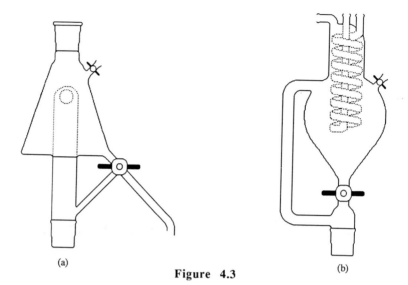

(a)

(b)

Figure 4.3

CHAPTER 5

Reagents: Purification and Handling

5.1 Introduction

One of the key steps to becoming a successful practitioner of modern organic chemistry is knowing how to handle and store air- and moisture-sensitive reagents, with the certainty that they have not been contaminated. This is a skill which takes some time to acquire and many people unfortunately learn the hard way, after a string of failed reactions. An efficient, successful organic chemist achieves good results rapidly, not by cutting corners, but by rigidly observing strict working practices that allow sensitive reagents to be used with confidence. The biggest waste of research time stems from employing reagents or procedures which you *think* are 'OK'. It will usually take far more time to repeat a reaction than it would have taken to re-purify a suspect reagent before starting. Perhaps more important than the time wasted by failed reactions, is the uncertainty which is introduced by using suspect reagents. No matter how carefully the outcome of an experimental reaction is quantified, in terms of yield, stereoselectivity, by-products, etc., the data will be meaningless if there was any uncertainty about the reaction conditions or reagents.

Handling sensitive reagents confidently is not difficult once a few standard techniques are learned and adhered to. In this chapter we will give examples of simple general methods which can be employed to handle a variety of reagents.

5.2   Classification of reagents for handling

The methods used to handle a particular reagent will be dependent on the properties of that reagent and you should be fully conversant with these before you start work. If you are working with a reagent and you are not familiar with its properties, you should look them up, or consult someone who is familiar with them, before you begin. This is very important, if you are to use the reagent effectively, without causing a hazard to you and others around you. Once you are conversant with the properties of a particular reagent, the handling requirements are largely a matter of common sense. For example, it is clearly unnecessary to rigorously exclude atmospheric moisture from a reagent which is to be reacted in aqueous solution, but it is important if the reagent is pyrophoric! Most reagents fall into one of the four categories below.

Stable non-toxic reagents

Reagents which are neither sensitive to the atmosphere nor toxic are normally stored in ordinary bottles on the shelf and they are usually easy to handle. However, if you are going to use this type of reagent for reactions with air sensitive materials, *they must also be dry and be stored with the atmosphere excluded!* It is no use setting up an anhydrous reaction very carefully, then adding a reagent straight from an unsealed bottle on the shelf.

Stable reagents which are toxic or have an unpleasant odour

These should be treated in the same way as those in the previous category, except that special precautions should be taken to avoid their escape into the lab. They should always be used in a fume cupboard and stored in a ventilated storage cupboard.

Reagents which will decompose on exposure to moisture or air

These reagents should always be stored in special containers, under a dry inert atmosphere. Whenever they are used, they should be measured and transferred using techniques which constantly maintain the inert atmosphere. Some of these techniques will be described below.

Reagents which decompose explosively or pyrophorically on exposure to moisture or air

These should be treated as above, but extra care should be taken, especially when dealing with residues once the reaction is over.

5.3 Techniques for obtaining pure and dry reagents

Before using any organic reagent or starting material for a reaction its purity should be checked. It should not be taken for granted that a reagent is pure simply because it has been obtained from a commercial source. Indeed the specification of many commercial compounds is much less than 100% and this should always be checked. Even if the specified purity of the reagent is high, at least one analytical check should also be carried out, such as tlc, gc or nmr. This check is particularly important if you are attempting new reactions. If the purity of the reagent is not up to the level required, standard purification techniques (distillation, recrystallization, chromatography, sublimation etc.) should be used to purify it (see Chapter 9 for more details).

Remember that any reagent which is to be used in a reaction under inert conditions with sensitive reagents, must also be dried very carefully!

Once you have gone to the trouble of purifying and drying a reagent, it is good practice to store it very carefully in order to keep it dry for future use. This normally means storing it in a sealed container, *under an inert atmosphere.* When you keep reagents in this way, you *must* be able to rely on their purity and it is therefore best to keep them for your own personal use. Remember that a person who has not gone to the trouble of purifying a reagent is not likely to take good care of yours!

In this section we will describe some typical techniques for purification and drying of reagents. There are several other more specialized texts which should be consulted if you need to purify other reagents.[1,2,3]

5.3.1 Purification and drying of liquids

For most liquids the method of choice for both purification and drying is distillation. In many cases the liquid is either dried over a drying agent before distillation or distilled from a drying agent (see also Chapter 4).

1. *Purification of Laboratory Chemicals*, 3rd ed., D.D. Perrin and W.L.F. Armarego, Pergamon Press, Oxford, 1988.
2. *Reagents for Organic Synthesis*, Vols. 1-13, Fieser and Fieser, Wiley, New York.
3. *Organic Synthesis*, Col. Vols. 1-6, Wiley, New York.

Distillation under inert atmosphere at normal pressure

This technique is used to purify and/or dry most liquid reagents which boil at less than about 150°C, at atmospheric pressure. Typically the liquid is pre-dried by shaking over magnesium sulphate, then decanted onto a more active drying agent, such as powdered calcium hydride, from which it is distilled. It is important to make sure that the drying agent does not react with the liquid. If you require a dry reagent, it is useless to carry out the distillation in the atmosphere, and the process must be carried out under argon (or nitrogen). For ease and reliability we suggest that a one-piece distillation apparatus is used for this type of distillation, in conjunction with a double manifold; the technique is fully described in Chapter 9, Section 9.4.2.

When the distillation is complete remove the collector, seal it quickly with a septum and purge the bottle with inert gas. For compounds which react with rubber, such as Lewis acids, a Teflon stopper should be used. Some of the less sensitive reagents can simply be poured into a reagent bottle before it is sealed, provided this is done quickly. However, if the reagent is particularly sensitive to air or moisture (such as a Lewis acid), a cannulation technique should be used to transfer it. See Section 5.4.1 for more details about storage and transfer of reagents under dry, inert conditions. Whatever type of container is used for storage it is always preferable that it be full, or nearly so.

Table 5.1

Reagent	Drying agent	b.p.°C	Comment
Methyl iodide	$CaCl_2$ before dist.	43	Very toxic! Wash with $Na_2S_2O_3$ or pour through alumina first to remove I_2
Diisopropylamine	dist. from CaH_2	84	
Triethylamine	dist. from CaH_2	89	
Isobutyraldehyde	$CaSO_4$ before dist.	62	readily oxidized
Titanium tetrachloride	none	136	very reactive with moisture
Cyclohexene	dist. from Na	83	wash first with $NaHSO_3$ to remove peroxides
Crotonaldehyde	$CaSO_4$ before dist.	104	use vigreux

Distillation under reduced pressure

For liquids with a high boiling point, or which decompose on heating, distillation under reduced pressure is the usual method of purification. Again it is convenient and effective to use a one-piece distillation apparatus in conjunction with a double manifold for this type of distillation. The procedure is described in more in Chapter 9, Section 9.4.2.

When the distillation is complete the heat is turned off and the two-way tap on the double manifold is slowly turned to the inert gas position. The flask containing the distillate will then be conveniently under an inert atmosphere and should be quickly removed and fitted with a tightly fitting septum (see Section 5.4.1 for more details about storing and transferring reagents under inert conditions).

Table 5.2

Reagent	Drying agent	b.p.°C/mm	Comment
Dimethyl formamide	$MgSO_4$ before dist.	76°/39	do not use CaH_2 or other basic drying agents
$BF_3.Et_2O$	dist. from CaH_2	67°/43	reacts with moisture
$SnCl_4$	dist. from tin	high vac.	reacts with moisture
Et_2AlCl	dist. from NaCl	107°/25	heated nichrome spiral in 50cm column; Reacts with air - spontaneously flammable!
Et_3Al	none	130°/55	*ibid.*
Benzaldehyde	$MgSO_4$ before dist.	62°/10	wash with Na_2CO_3 before dist. Store over 0.1% hydroquinone
Benzyl bromide	$MgSO_4$ before dist.	85°/12	dist. in dark. *lacrymator*

Some special cases for drying of liquids

There are a number of liquid reagents which hydrolyse when they come in contact with water and subsequently contain the hydrolysis product, which is usually an acid. These reagents are distilled from a high-boiling amine, or other base, so that any acidic impurity is removed. It is always important that the distillation is carried out under inert atmosphere (or under reduced pressure) and the techniques are exactly as above. Some examples are given in Table 5.3.

Table 5.3

Reagent	Distil from	b.p.°C	Comment
Acetic anhydride	quinoline	138	10:1 with quinoline
Acetyl chloride	quinoline	52	10:1 with quinoline
Me_3SiCl^*	quinoline	106	10:1 with quinoline
(Chloro trimethylsilane)			

*Another method for removing HCl from trimethylsilyl chloride (chlorotrimethyl silane) is to add it to an equal volume of triethylamine in a centrifuge tube, sealed under argon with a septum. After centrifuging, triethylamine hydrochloride forms a solid precipitate and the liquid can be drawn off by syringe and used for most purposes as 50% Me_3SiCl.

Details about how to store and handle liquid reagents under dry and inert conditions are given in Section 5.4.1.

5.3.2 Purifying and drying solid reagents

If the purity of the reagent is not up to the level required, standard solid purification techniques (chromatography, recrystallization, sublimation) should be used to purify it (see Chapter 9 for more details).

Remember that if a solid reagent is to be used in a reaction under inert conditions with sensitive reagents, it must be dried very carefully. For bulk drying of solids an oven is often used (preferably a vacuum oven), or the solid is placed in a vacuum desiccator over a drying agent (P_2O_5, H_2SO_4, etc.). If the reagent is to be stored, for future use in reactions under inert conditions, it should be kept under argon (or nitrogen), in a sealed bottle, to prevent exposure to moisture. Small quantities of solid can often be dried in the reaction flask, prior to the apparatus being set up. This is conveniently done by connecting the dried flask, containing the solid, to the double manifold, evacuating under high vacuum for several hours, then introducing argon (or nitrogen).

Purification of some common solid reagents

AIBN (α,α'-Azobis(isobutyronitrile))

Recrystallize from ether and dry under vacuum, over P_2O_5 at room temperature. Store under inert atmosphere, in the dark, at -10°C.

Para-toluenesulphonyl chloride

Para -toluenesulphonyl chloride often contains a considerable quantity of p-toluenesulphonic acid. This can be removed by placing the reagent in the thimble of a soxhlet apparatus containing dry petroleum ether. After several hours of extraction under an inert atmosphere, the chloride will have dissolved in the solvent and the unwanted acid will be left behind in the soxhlet thimble. On cooling the solvent mixture, the acid chloride crystallizes and can be collected by filtration. The purified material should be stored under an inert atmosphere.

Copper(I) iodide (for the preparation of cuprate reagents)

Impure copper iodide is often slightly brown due to the presence of iodine and copper(II) salts. It is very important that these contaminants are removed and that the reagent is dried efficiently if it is to be used in the preparation of copper-lithium reagents. This is accomplished by placing the material in the thimble of a soxhlet apparatus and extracting with methylene chloride for several hours (usually overnight) until no further colour is being removed. The almost white reagent is then dried under vacuum and stored under argon (or nitrogen) in a dark bottle, sealed with parafilm.

Magnesium (for Grignard reactions etc.)

Wash with ether, to remove grease from the surface of the metal, dry at 100°C under vacuum and cool in a desiccator. For a more active form of magnesium, stir the turnings under nitrogen overnight. They will turn almost black as the oxide coat is removed from the surface. The material produced is very active and should be stored under inert atmosphere.

Zinc

Zinc is normally coated with oxide, which must be removed prior to use. This can be done by stirring with 10% HCl for 2 min, then filtering and washing with water, followed by acetone. The metal can then be vacuum-dried and kept under an inert atmosphere prior to use.

5.4   Techniques for handling and measuring reagents

Although extreme care must be taken to exclude air and moisture from reagents kept under an inert atmosphere, once you become familiar with the simple techniques outlined in this section, you should find them easy to use. Bottles and flasks containing liquids or solutions sealed under an inert atmosphere are widely used in modern organic chemistry. A knowledge of the techniques required to manipulate such reagents, without allowing them to come into contact with the atmosphere, is therefore essential.

When handling air sensitive reagents always *think ahead, and design the whole sequence of events you intend to follow so that air never comes into contact with the reagent.*

A method for titration of alkyllithium reagents is given in Chapter 16 and a method for titration of hydride reagents is given in Chapter 6.

5.4.1 Storing liquid reagents or solvents under an inert atmosphere

After drying and/or distillation, reagents or solvents can be stored, under argon, in a bottle or flask sealed with a septum. There are also many other commonly used reagents that are extremely reactive towards water and/or oxygen and these are stored in the same way. Examples of such reagents are: alkyllithium reagents; Grignard reagents; organoboranes; metal hydrides; organoaluminium compounds and Lewis acids. Some of these are available commercially and are delivered under inert atmosphere in sealed bottles. Less common reagents may be prepared in the lab and then stored for future use. The seals of the commercially supplied containers have a limited life-span and if one is suspect it should be replaced with a rubber septum. For Lewis acids, which often react with rubber, a Teflon stopper can be used. For storing small quantities of liquid under inert atmosphere 'mininert valves' are very useful. These screw threaded bottle caps incorporate Teflon valves through which a syringe needle can enter the container. They provide a better seal than ordinary septa (see Section 5.4.4 for more detail on the use of mininert valves).

To change or fit a septum

Choose a septum which fits tightly into the neck of the bottle that you wish to seal. Fit a new septum as quickly as possible, minimizing exposure of the reagent to the atmosphere. As soon as the septum has been fitted purge the container with argon (or nitrogen). This is done using a syringe needle connected to an inert gas manifold by a Luer adapter. Another needle is used as a vent as shown in Fig. 5.1a. The septum should be secured with copper wire and for extra protection another septum of the same size, without any needle holes in it, can be pulled over the first (Fig. 5.1b and c). The second septum is removed before syringing liquid from the bottle. For long term storage, it is also a good idea to wrap parafilm around the septum, especially if the bottle is to be stored in the fridge.

Figure 5.1

If the septum has been fitted properly and the reagent is used carefully, according to the techniques below, it can be kept for many months and used many times over.

If you need to use a reagent which has been stored in a fridge or freezer, always allow it to warm up to room temperature and remove any condensation, before unsealing it.

5.4.2 Bulk transfer of a liquid under inert atmosphere (cannulation)

As a general rule, never attempt to remove liquid from a container which is sealed under inert gas, unless you have pressurized the container with inert gas first (Fig. 5.2a). Also, whenever you are using ground glass joints connected under pressure always secure them with either plastic (bibby) clips, elastic bands or springs.

General principle of cannulation and gas pressure adjustments

Cannulation is a very general procedure for the transfer of a liquid from one container to another whilst maintaining an inert atmosphere. The principle of cannulation is very simple. A positive pressure is applied to the flask from which the liquid is to be transferred. This pressure forces the liquid out through a double ended needle (cannula) into the receiving flask (see Fig. 5.3). In order for the liquid to flow, there must be some means by which the gas in the receiving vessel can escape. The simplest way to allow this to happen is to vent the receiving flask with a short needle passed through the septum. It is good practice to connect the vent needle to a bubbler to prevent suck back of air occurring.

It is is quite common that the flask into which you need to cannulate the liquid is already part of an inert gas system and can not simply be vented. In this case the pressure applied to the first flask must be higher than the pressure in the receiving flask if the liquid is to flow and *there must be some means by which gas can escape from the receiving flask.* All inert gas systems should incorporate a bubbler (for example, see Fig. 3.7) and this automatically provides a means of escape for gas which is displaced from the receiving flask. To create a higher pressure in the delivery flask, the inert gas inlet could, in principle, be connected directly to a cylinder outlet. However, it is preferable to incorporate a bubbler into this line also. The rate of flow of liquid during cannulation will be governed by the pressure in this gas line and it can easily be controlled by restricting the vent of the bubbler with a finger. For more precise control of pressure the vent can be restricted by connecting a Rotaflow tap or needle valve to it (see Fig. 5.2).

General procedure for cannulation

The following procedure is a general method for transferring liquids by cannulation and will be referred to in other sections of the book.

1. Make sure the bottle or flask into which you are going to transfer the reagent is thoroughly dry, fit a septum into the neck and purge with inert gas as described in the previous section. If the container was oven dried it is preferable to fit the septum whilst it is still hot and allow it to cool as it is being purged with inert gas (Fig. 5.1a).

2. When the bottle or flask is cool, make sure the septum is fitted tightly and wire it on, then remove the vent *before removing* the argon line

(Fig.5.1b). The container now contains an inert atmosphere and is ready for use.

3. Insert an inert gas line needle into the septum of the bottle or flask containing the liquid to be transferred. If you are transferring liquid to a flask that is already part of an inert gas system, a separate gas line must be used to pressurize the bottle and a simple bubbler system is recommended (Fig. 5.2a).

inert gas
from cylinder →

restrict vent →
with finger or
needle valve
to increase
pressure

(a)   (b)

Figure 5.2

4. Insert a double ended needle (cannula) into the bottle containing the reagent, *taking care not to push the needle below the surface of the liquid.* Check that the inert gas is flowing through the system and out through the cannula (Fig. 5.2b).

5. Insert the other end of the cannula through the septum of the new bottle or flask, then push the inlet end below the surface of the liquid in the delivery flask. There should be no flow initially, because the receiving container is sealed. Vent it by inserting a short needle through the septum. The vent needle can be connected to a bubbler or an inert gas system which incorporates a bubbler. If the liquid does not start to flow, increase the pressure by restricting the vent of the inlet bubbler using a finger, a septum or by connecting a needle valve (Fig. 5.3). When argon is used it is normally safe to dispense with the bubbler connected to the vent of the collecting flask.

inert gas
from cylinder→

restrict vent→
with finger or
needle valve
to increase
pressure

→ vent to
bubbler or
to inert gas
system that
incorporates
a bubbler

Figure 5.3

6. When all the liquid has been transferred, first remove the vent needle, then remove the cannula at the receiver end. The remainder of the system can then be dismantled in any order, but remember to be very careful with the residues, particularly if the liquid is toxic or reactive to moisture.

5.4.3   Using cannulation techniques to transfer measured volumes of liquid under inert atmosphere

The cannulation technique can easily be adapted for measuring volumes of liquid under inert atmosphere. It is mainly used for measuring quantities of liquid that are too large to be conveniently handled by syringe (> 50ml), but it is also suitable for measuring pre-cooled solutions without significant warming. The cannulation technique is identical to that described in the previous section, but an intermediary graduated container is used. The graduated container can be a measuring cylinder with a neck that can be fitted with a septum (Fig. 5.4a), or it can be a graduated Schlenk tube (Fig. 5.4b).

Dry the container and transfer the required quantity of liquid to it according to the procedure described in Section 5.4.2.

Once the required volume of liquid has been measured, remove the needle from the storage bottle and insert it through the septum of a dry receiving vessel that is filled with inert gas. Apply inert gas pressure to the graduated cylinder and vent the receiving flask to deliver the liquid (Fig. 5.5, see also Chapter 8 for more details on setting up reactions).

Figure 5.4

Figure 5.5

If the liquid is being measured for addition to a reaction flask, an alternative procedure is to use a graduated pressure equalizing dropping funnel attached to the apparatus. The required quantity of liquid can then be cannulated into the dropping funnel directly.

Types of cannula

For most purposes cannulation can be carried out using an ordinary double ended needle, bent to a suitable shape (Fig. 5.6a). A cannula made by joining two long syringe needles to a Luer to Luer stopcock allows the flow of liquid to be controlled (Fig. 5.6b). For tansferring large volumes of liquid the 'flex-needle' (available from Aldrich Chemical Co.) is useful. This is a jacketed Teflon tube with a wide-bore needle attached to either end (Fig. 5.6c). It provides rapid liquid transfer, and a degree of insulation for a cold reagent. The wide-bore needles of the flex-needle should not be inserted through a new septum without first making a hole with a normal gauge needle.

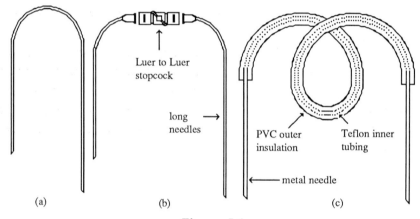

Figure 5.6

For small scale work all Teflon cannulas are very useful, and some people prefer them to syringes. They are easily made by taking a piece of narrow-bore (1.5mm) Teflon tubing, of a suitable length and cutting each end at a shallow angle with a sharp razor blade or scalpel (Fig. 5.7). Always be sure to make holes in the septa, using a metal needle, before attempting to insert the Teflon cannula.

Figure 5.7

5.4.4 Use of syringes for the transfer of reagents or solvents

Syringes are extremely useful for transferring small quantities (up to 50ml) of air sensitive reagents or dry solvents from one bottle or flask to another. There are a variety of syringe types and you need to appreciate which type is suitable for a particular application. It is most important to choose a syringe of an appropriate size for the quantity of liquid you need to transport. Using a syringe with a volume much larger than you need will lead to inaccuracy and using a syringe which is too small will waste time. For most purposes the syringe should be equipped with a long needle (10-20cm). This is necessary in order to avoid any need to tip the reagent or solvent bottle when syringing from it. When using syringes, the condition of septa should be checked regularly. Their life can be extended by making sure that the needle tips are kept sharp.

The skill of using syringes is of great importance to an organic chemist, but, as with all skills, you will only become proficient after a certain amount of practice. It is a good idea to have your own set of syringes which are appropriate for the type of work in which you are engaged. They will be some of your most frequently used tools so you should practice using them and take great care of them.

Types of syringe

Micro syringes

Micro syringes are extremely useful for small scale synthetic work, delivering small quantities of liquid accurately. Sizes ranging from $10\mu l$ to 1ml are common, but $100\mu l$ is perhaps the most useful size to have.

There are two general types of micro syringe, gas-tight and liquid-tight. The liquid-tight syringes have matched glass bores and stainless steel plungers, which should not be mixed-up (Fig. 5.8). Certain types of reagent will corrode the steel plunger and cause ceasure if the syringe is not cleaned immediately after use. These are indeed delicate and quite expensive items which should always be treated with great care (see later for care of syringes).

glass barrel   matched metal plunger

screw-on needle

Figure 5.8

Gas-tight micro syringes have Teflon tipped plungers, making them more inert to chemical reagents (e.g. Lewis acids). The barrels and plungers are also interchangeable and they are thus much more reliable than the liquid-tight syringes. The drawback with gas tight syringes is that they are more expensive (Fig. 5.9).

glass barrel   Teflon tipped plunger

screw-on needle

Figure 5.9

Both types of micro syringe are available with either fixed or removable needles, but the type with removable needles are generally preferred. Removable needles have the advantages that they can be replaced when damaged or blocked and that different sizes can be fitted. Long needles for micro syringes normally have to be ordered specially.

All-glass Luer syringes

These syringes range in size from 1ml to 100ml, are generally quite cheap and are the most commonly used type. Some glass syringes have matched barrel and plunger and they can only be used as a pair, but most modern syringes have interchangeable barrels and plungers. Syringes with interchangeable parts will be marked as such and these are the preferred type to use. They are adequate for most purposes, but should be cleaned immediately after use and treated carefully to avoid jamming.

glass plunger   glass barrel

Figure 5.10

Glass gas-tight Luer syringes

For most purposes these are the best type of syringe available. The barrel of the syringe is made from glass and the plunger is made from metal or plastic and has a separate Teflon tip (Fig. 5.11). Their main advantages over all-glass syringes are that they are less prone to leakage and jamming. They are very expensive, but all the components are replaceable, so they do last a long time.

plunger with Teflon tip   glass barrel

Figure 5.11

Plastic disposable syringes

Plastic syringes are cheap, hold a very good seal, they are quite accurate and virtually unbreakable. They can be used many times over, but they do have the drawback of being susceptible to attack from certain solvents. For this reason they are most widely used transferring aqueous solutions, such as aqueous hydrogen peroxide.

Syringe fittings

Micro syringes normally have one of two types of screw-on needle, as shown in Figs. 5.8 and 5.9. The fittings of larger syringes are more standard and are normally the Luer type. A Luer fitting is a joint produced with a standard taper which matches the internal taper of a Luer syringe needle. There are several types of Luer fitting (Fig. 5.12).

Luer tip -
steel or Teflon

locking sleeve

Luer lock   metal Luer   glass Luer

Figure 5.12

The simplest fitting is the Luer glass tip, but these break very easily and should be avoided. Metal Luer tips are more robust, but the needles tend to work loose and for this reason Luer-lock syringes are preferred. These have a slot into which the rim of the needle engages so that it can not come loose. The most common fitting is the metal tip Luer-lock, but the best seal of all is provided by the Teflon tip Luer-lock, normally found only on gas-tight syringes. In this case the Luer tip is Teflon and the locking sleeve is metal.

Syringe needles

Luer fitting syringe needles are available in a range of lengths and bore diameters. The optimum bore diameter depends on the volume of liquid being dispensed. As a rough guide we use 22 gauge needles for volumes of less than 1ml, 20 gauge for volumes between 1 to 5ml and 18 gauge for larger quantities. Long needles are usually preferred for transferring liquids by syringe, but short needles are useful as nitrogen inlets or vents. Disposable needles with plastic shanks can also be used for this purpose.

Bevel must be clean and sharp

long all-metal needle for transferring liquid

short disposable needle for introducing and venting inert gas

Figure 5.13

Most needles have a 12° bevel and this should be kept in good, sharp condition so that minimal damage is caused when penetrating a septum. Flat ended needles are sometimes useful for removing the last traces of liquid from a container, but they should only be introduced through septa which have previously been pierced by a sharp needle.

Cleaning and care of syringes

Syringes and needles can give good service for long periods, but careful treatment is required to prevent leakage and jamming. It is therefore very important to clean syringes and needles *immediately* after use. Organic liquids or solutions are generally quite easily removed, by simply flushing with solvent. However, more care is required when a reactive reagent such as butyllithium or titanium tetrachloride has been used. To clear such reactive reagents the syringe should *immediately* be flushed several times with the solvent in which the reagent is dissolved. Whatever the syringe has been used for it should *always* be dismantled for final cleaning of the individual components. If the syringe has been used for an alkyllithium or any other strongly basic reagent, it should be washed with dilute HCl, water, then acetone. After using an acidic reagent or a Lewis acid, the components should be washed with dilute sodium hydroxide, water, then acetone.

If a syringe has jammed or become contaminated with remnants of a stubborn reagent, handle it carefully and *do not use force* to free the plunger. This will almost certainly lead to the syringe being broken and you may well end up with a cut hand also. One of the most reliable methods for removing a contaminant from a syringe, or syringe needle, is to submerge it in a solvent which will dissolve the contaminant and place it in an ultra sonic cleaning bath for a few minutes. Sonication will often free syringes which are completely jammed provided you choose the correct solvent. If you do not know what is blocking the syringe try sequentially sonicating in the following series of solvents; 10% HCl, then water, then dilute NaOH, then water, then acetone, then methanol and finally methylene chloride.

How to handle a syringe

The type of reagent that you will need to deliver by syringe is very often one that has to be measured precisely in order for the reaction to be successful. It is also likely to be a very corrosive reagent, such as butyllithium, which you do not want to splash around the lab or spill onto your skin. So, before attempting to use a syringe for transferring any reagent, practise using it first by measuring solvent until you are confident that you can handle it safely. You will often need to hold a syringe full of liquid in one hand whilst performing another operation with the other hand. One way to do this is as follows: fill the syringe with the required volume of liquid using both hands; then place the syringe against the palm of one hand using the 3rd, 4th and 5th fingers of the same hand to grip the barrel; carefully place the forefinger around the plunger and against the end of the barrel to hold the plunger firmly in place; the liquid can now be delivered by pressing the plunger down using the thumb, and the other hand is completely free. This method should be practised using solvent until your technique is good enough to confidently transfer liquid without spillage.

Preparing a syringe for use

An appropriate clean syringe and needle should be chosen, dried in an oven, then left to cool in a desiccator. Before using a syringe it should be purged with argon (or nitrogen) and this is conveniently done by 'syringing out' the gas *via* a septum inlet attached to the inert gas system. This should be repeated several times (Fig. 5.14). After purging with argon (or nitrogen) the syringe can be kept for a short time before use if the tip of the needle is inserted into a rubber stopper.

Figure 5.14

Syringing liquid from a bottle or flask under inert atmosphere

Before attempting to syringe liquid from a bottle which is under an inert atmosphere, make sure you have: an effective inert gas system with a needle outlet; a dry syringe (and preferably a spare) prepared as described above; and a receptacle, *also under inert conditions*, into which you are going to transfer the liquid. The procedure outlined below should be practised with solvent first if you have not done it before.

1. Pressurize the reagent container with an inert gas line using a syringe needle attached *via* a tubing connector.
2. Carefully insert the needle of the syringe through the septum, holding the syringe plunger in. Then *very slowly* fill the syringe by pulling the plunger up (Fig. 5.15a). You should never fill the syringe more than about two-thirds capacity.
3. Tip the syringe upside down, bending the long needle. Slowly force any excess reagent and bubbles back into the bottle until the exact volume is indicated (Fig. 5.15b).
4. Holding the syringe barrel carefully in place with one hand, slowly withdraw the needle from the septum using your other hand to control it. Then, avoiding prolonged exposure to the atmosphere, *quickly* insert the needle into the receptor.
5. Slowly deliver the measured volume into the receptor flask, which should itself be connected to an inert gas system.

Figure 5.15

Syringing reagents which are extremely moisture sensitive

When a particularly moisture sensitive reagent is being transported by syringe, simply exposing the tip of the syringe needle to the atmosphere may cause problems. However, there is a very simple method for keeping the syringe tip under inert atmosphere at all times. Take a short piece of dry glass tubing (about 5cm long), insert a tight fitting septum in each end and purge with inert gas. This provides a mobile inert gas capsule that can be used to protect your syringe tip (Fig. 5.16a). The procedure for transferring the liquid is exactly as described above except for the following points:

1. When drawing the liquid out of the reagent container the syringe needle is passed through both septa of the inert gas capsule (Fig. 5.16b).

2. After filling the syringe the end of the needle is pulled into the capsule so that the tip is protected (Fig. 5.16c).

3. The capsule is pressed against the septum of the receiving flask and the needle is pushed through both septa to deliver the liquid (Fig. 5.16d).

Figure 5.16

Syringing from Mininert bottles

Mininert valves are too narrow for two syringe needles to pass through them. It is therefore impossible for a container fitted with a Mininert valve to be pressurized from an inert gas system while syringing from it. However, because the containers used with these valves are very small a very simple alternative procedure can be used.

1. After flushing a syringe with inert gas fill it with slightly more gas than the quantity of liquid you wish to syringe. (A gas-tight syringe is preferred for this procedure).
2. Open the Mininert valve, push the syringe needle through and push the plunger to pressurize the container with inert gas.
3. With the needle below the surface of the liquid allow the syringe to fill with liquid, under the pressure which you have introduced (never suck liquid into the syringe as this will draw air into the system).
4. Bend the needle to invert the syringe, displace air bubbles and measure the required volume of liquid.
5. Remove the needle from the container and deliver the liquid as usual.

5.4.5 Handling and weighing solids under inert atmosphere

Manipulation of solid reagents under dry conditions tends to be somewhat more awkward than handling liquids or solutions. However, there are two distinctly different problems which can be considered. Firstly, there is the use of dry but unreactive solid reagents in reactions under inert conditions, and this will be dealt with in Chapter 8. The other, and more significant problem, is manipulation of very reactive solid reagents which may react with moisture in the atmosphere. The only way to handle solids under completely dry conditions is to use a glove box, which is a sophisticated and relatively expensive piece of equipment. Fortunately most solid reagents used in organic chemistry are not so reactive that absolute dryness is required.

In cases where great accuracy is required, or where a particularly reactive solid is to be handled, a glove bag can be used. This is essentially a large, clear polythene bag, which can be sealed after equipment and reagents have been placed in it. Inlets are provided for electricity cables, gas lines etc. and glove inserts allow for the manipulation of the apparatus inside the bag. After loading all the equipment and the reagent into the bag, it is evacuated three times and filled with an inert gas (a double manifold can be used for this purpose). Some skill is required to work within a glove bag so, as usual when working under inert conditions, plan your work very carefully making sure everything you require is on hand before you start. It is also a good idea to practice working in the bag before you attempt the 'real thing'.

In the vast majority of cases, the reactive solids used in organic synthesis can be handled relatively simply, without the need for a glove bag, provided you master a few simple techniques, and you are careful and work quickly. The most common moisture sensitive solids are metals (sodium, lithium, potassium etc.) and metal hydrides (sodium hydride, potassium hydride, lithium aluminium hydride etc.) and the most commonly encountered problem is weighing. We have already seen that measuring liquids under inert atmosphere is relatively simple and for this reason many air-sensitive organic solids are sold in solution. In order to weigh a solid without using a glove bag, a certain amount of exposure to the atmosphere is inevitable, but this can be minimized, provided you are careful. When carrying out a reaction it is normally best if you can plan events so that any air sensitive solid is added to the reaction flask before other reagents or solvent (see Chapter 8 for more details).

Weighing solid reactive metals

As usual, plan your work ahead and make sure you have a flask pre-dried and under inert gas. The metal will normally be under paraffin oil and may also have an oxide or hydroxide layer coating it. Both these impurities will have to be removed before weighing the metal and this can be done using the following sequence. *Remember that reactive metals are pyrophoric when they come into contact with moisture.*

1. Place the metal into a beaker, covering it with oil, then cut some of it into small pieces with a scalpel, removing any coating and leaving the shiny surface exposed. *Heavily coated potassium has been known to detonate on cutting and should be discarded.*

2. Using a pair of forceps, quickly wash the oil from the metal chunks in a second beaker containing *dry* hexane or pentane. Remove the chunks, allowing the solvent to evaporate very briefly, and drop into a weighed beaker of oil.

3. Once you have weighed the required quantity, remove the metal chunks, wash again in the pet. ether, quickly add them to the reaction flask and re-connect to the inert gas system.

4. When weighing is complete add an alcohol (e.g. ethanol) to the beakers to neutralize any scraps of metal before washing with water.

i) clean metal   ii) wash   iii) weigh into a beaker
   and cut   of oil, then re-wash

Figure 5.17

Handling metal and metal hydride dispersions

Finely divided metals and metal hydrides are very useful reagents and are usually packed as dispersions in paraffin oil. The most common of these reagents are sodium hydride, potassium hydride and lithium metal. Whilst dispersed in the oil the reagents are moderately stable and can be weighed out quickly in the atmosphere.

For some experiments the dispersion can be used without separating out the oil. To do this simply weight it into a pre-dried reaction flask and place it under inert atmosphere by sequentially evacuating, then purging the flask with an inert gas. A 3-way Quickfit tap connected to a double manifold is ideal for this purpose.

There are various techniques for removing the oil from a metal dispersion. The simplest method is as follows:

1. Weigh the dispersion in a flask (do not forget to take the oil into account) and place it under inert atmosphere. Use a double manifold connected by a 3-way Quickfit tap if possible (Fig. 5.18a).

2. While maintaining a rapid flow of inert gas through the bubbler of the inert gas system, open the 3-way tap and add some dry petroleum ether using a syringe. Swirl the flask to dissolve the oil, then let it stand until the metal has settled at the bottom (Fig. 5.18b).

Figure 5.18

3. Draw off the petroleum ether carefully using a syringe (Fig. 5.18c). Discard the solvent carefully as it may contain a small quantity of the metal.

4. Repeat the washing process two more times.

5. The flask can then be evacuated to remove last traces of petroleum ether, then re-weighed to determine the exact quantity of metal.

Reaction solvents and other reagents can then be added directly to this flask.

If you need to separate the oil from a quantity of metal dispersion without placing it directly into a reaction flask, the piece of apparatus shown in Fig. 5.19 is very useful. A typical procedure is as follows:

1. After drying the filtration apparatus and cooling under a stream of inert gas, quickly weigh into it slightly more than the required quantity of the dispersion, loosely packed.

2. Add some *dry* petroleum ether to the apparatus and quickly connect a Quickfit 3-way Teflon tap to the top.

3. Open the stopcock at the bottom of the funnel and pressurize with inert gas (Fig. 5.19a). The inert gas can be introduced from a simple line which incorporates a bubbler (see Fig. 5.2a). The vent of the bubbler should be restricted to increase the pressure.

Figure 5.19

4. Before the level of the solvent reaches the top of the dispersion, turn the the 3-way tap so that argon is directed out of the vertical inlet as well as

into the funnel. Then add more solvent through the vent using a Pasteur pipette (Fig. 5.19b).

5. Repeat the washing steps until solvent flows freely, indicating that all the oil has been washed away, then close the top and bottom stopcocks.

This procedure will leave you with finely divided metal or hydride, under argon, and this can be kept for a few hours in the sealed apparatus without deterioration. The fine powder will be very reactive and therefore great care is required in handling it. For titration of metal hydrides see Chapter 6.

Weighing reactive powdered solids

The simple procedure given below can be used for most solids, other than those which are extremely reactive with even the slightest amount of moisture or air. Examples of reagents which can be weighed by this method are: sodium hydride, potassium hydride, lithium metal, lithium aluminium hydride, finely divided metals and metal hydrides (from dispersions). A glove bag should be used for particularly reactive solids, or in cases where extreme accuracy is required.

As always, plan ahead when handling reactive materials and make sure you have a dry vessel, under inert atmosphere, into which you want to weigh the powder.

1. Remove the receiving vessel from the inert gas system and place on a balance pan under a stream of argon, provided by the simple set-up shown in Fig. 5.20. *Caution: argon is the preferred inert gas for this procedure, but because it is heavier than air, make sure the flask remains filled through-out the weighing procedure.*

2. Keep the top of the container holding the powdered metal under the argon stream whilst removing it, and quickly weigh the required amount into the flask. ***When weighing any finely powdered reactive solid avoid sifting it through the air as this can lead to a fire.***

3. Re-connect the flask to the inert gas system (preferably a double manifold, evacuate very carefully to avoid the power being disturbed, then refill with inert gas.

4. Carefully neutralize remaining traces of the metal or hydride on the apparatus using an alcohol.

← argon

← filter funnel

balance

Figure 5.20

The inverted filter funnel technique described above reduces contact of the reactive solid with moist air and thus lowers the chances of deterioration, and also the risk of fire. In some instances the less reactive powders, such as sodium hydride, can be safely weighed in the atmosphere if you are quick and careful. However, it is recommend that an inert atmosphere blanket is always used for weighing more reactive reagents, such as potassium hydride.

5.5   Preparation of diazomethane

Diazomethane is an extremely valuable reagent which is very easy to prepare and use. However, there are certain hazards associated with the compound and its preparation that should be taken into account. The observance of a few simple safety measures allow the reagent to be prepared and used with confidence.

The single most valuable application of diazomethane is its reaction with carboxylic acids to provide the equivalent methyl ester, under very mild conditions. This and other reactions of the reagent have been well reviewed.[4]

4. T.H. Black, *Aldrichimica Acta*, 1983, **16**, 3.

5.5.1 Safety measures

There are two types of hazard associated with diazomethane; toxicity and detonation. Since the reagent is a gas, it can easily be inhaled causing serious lung disorders and a cancer risk. The precursors to diazomethane are also toxic and should also be treated with extreme care.

Diazomethane has been known to explode, initiators to detonation being rough glass surfaces, alkali metals, certain drying agents such as calcium sulphate, and strong light.

Fortunately, the risks highlighted can be circumvented by adhering to the following simple safety measures.

1. *Diazomethane should always be prepared and used in an efficient fume cupboard, behind a safety shield.*
2. *The detonation risk is chiefly associated with concentrated solutions or neat diazomethane, and the risk is almost completely avoided if it is always handled in dilute solution. This also reduces the health hazard.*
3. *Never use diazomethane with ground glass joints or glass apparatus with rough, broken edges and do not use anti bumping chips.*
4. *If a dry solution is required use potassium hydroxide as the drying agent.*
5. *Avoid strong light.*
6. *Do not store diazomethane, use it immediately and neutralize any excess reagent with acetic acid.*

5.5.2 Preparation of diazomethane (a dilute ethereal solution)

'Clearfit' apparatus can be used to prepare diazomethane, but a cheaper alternative is to have a simple one piece distillation apparatus made by a glassblower. The set-up shown in Fig. 5.21 can be used to prepare between 3 and 17mmol of diazomethane.

Figure 5.21

Method 1

Dissolve KOH (1g) in water (2ml), dilute with 95% ethanol (8ml), and add to the reaction flask. Cool the flask in an ice bath, then slowly add a solution of Diazald (*N*-methyl-*N*-nitroso-*p*-toluenesuphonamide) in diethyl ether (15ml), using a Pasteur pipette. When all the Diazald has been added, stopper the neck of the flask, put the ice bath under the receiver and place a warm water bath (about 65°C) under the reaction flask. The yellow diazomethane-ether mixture will start to distil out of the flask. Carry-on distilling until all the yellow colour has disappeared from the reaction flask, adding a further 5ml of diethyl ether if necessary. The yellow distillate contains about 3.3mmol of diazomethane.

Method 2

To produce 16.6mmol of diazomethane use 5g Diazald, 5g KOH, 8ml water, 10ml ethanol and 50ml of diethyl ether. The procedure is similar, but on this larger scale, add the Diazald solution slowly to the warm KOH solution, while distilling off the diazomethane. A separating funnel (with a PTFE stopcock) pushed through a rubber stopper can be used for the addition.

5.5.3 General procedure for esterification of carboxylic acids

To an ice cooled solution of the carboxylic acid in ether or ethanol, add an ethereal solution of diazomethane slowly, until gas evolution stops, and a very pale yellow colour remains. Add just enough dilute acetic acid in ether to remove the yellow colour, then evaporate the mixture and purify the product as appropriate. For very acid-sensitive reactants the acetic acid work-up can be omitted, and excess diazomethane removed by bubbling nitrogen through the reaction mixture (in a good fume cupboard) until all the yellow colour has disappeared.

5.5.4 Titration of diazomethane solutions

Add an aliquot of diazomethane solution to an accurately weighed, excess quantity of benzoic acid in ether. Dilute the mixture with ether and titrate with a standard alkali solution to calculate the quantity of acid remaining.

For more information on the uses of diazomethane see reference 4.

CHAPTER 6

Gases

6.1 Introduction

Many organic reactions require the use of gases, either inert gases which are used to protect the reaction, or reagent gases which actually take part in the reaction. Special experimental techniques are required for handling gases and this chapter contains a summary of methods for the preparation, handling and measurement of the more commonly encountered gases.

It must be emphasized at the outset that many gases are very hazardous, either because they are toxic or because they are supplied in cylinders which contain compressed gas at very high pressures and, as a result, particular attention must be paid to safe practice in gas manipulation.

6.2 Use of gas cylinders

A large number of gases are commercially available and details about individual gases are provided in Sections 6.5 and 6.6. The purpose of this section is to describe safe methods for handling the containers in which these gases are supplied.[1,2]

Most gases are supplied in pressurized metal cylinders in sizes ranging from about 50cm in diameter and 350cm tall (lecture bottles) to the familiar size used for nitrogen (ca. 0.25m diameter by 1.5m tall). Some gases with higher boiling points are supplied at lower pressure in relatively light metal cylinders. The fittings on the cylinders vary depending on the supplier and

1. *Safe under Pressure,* BOC Ltd, 1988.
2. *Handbook of Compressed Gases,* Compressed Gas Association, Reinhold, 1981.

on the gas hence it is very important to comply with the suppliers instructions regarding fittings and accessories.

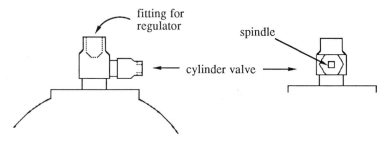

Figure 6.1

Most cylinders are fitted with a unit containing an on-off valve, and an outlet fitting (Fig. 6.1). *This unit should never be tampered with.* The valve fitting is a weak point in the cylinder and might be dislodged or weakened if the cylinder was dropped. Apart from releasing a potentially dangerous gas this could allow the highly pressurized gas to vent uncontrollably converting the cylinder into an extremely dangerous missile.

For this reason cylinders and lecture bottles should never be allowed to stand unsupported.

They should always be securely clamped to a bench or a wall. If they have to be moved frequently they should be supported in a sturdy metal frame, or in a trolley designed for this purpose. Cylinders should only be moved in purpose designed trolleys and should always be treated with great care.

Cylinders are generally pressurized to 175-200atm and the on/off valves provide no more control than their name suggests so cylinders must be fitted with a regulator to allow controlled delivery of the gas. The most popular regulators are the two stage types shown in Fig. 6.2.

The regulators provide a constant *outlet pressure* which can be adjusted to suit the particular application. These are often fitted with needle valves to give control over the *outlet flow rate*. The procedure for fitting a regulator to a cylinder is as follows:

1. Find the correct regulator for the gas in question. Different gas cylinders have different fittings (to prevent the gas from coming into

output pressure gauge

cylinder pressure gauge

needle valve

pressure adjusting screw

Figure 6.2

contact with incompatible materials) so the appropriate regulator, fitted with the correct threaded connector, must be used. (Consult supplier's data for more detailed information). For safety reasons it is best to choose a regulator which has a fairly low delivery pressure ($\leq$ 0-50 psi), unless a high output pressure is specifically required. (1atm = 1.01bar = 14.5psi (lbf/in^2) = 1.03 kgf/cm^2 = 760mmHg.)

2. Remove the protective cap from the cylinder fitting and ensure that the fitting is clean and dry.
   Never use grease or Teflon tape on cylinder fittings.

3. Screw the fitting onto the cylinder and tighten firmly. A poor fit probably means that the regulator is not of the correct type. (Note that some cylinders have 'left hand' threads.)
   Never try to force the fitting.

4. Test for leaks by applying a little dilute soapy water, or a commercial leak detection solution, around the joint.

The correct procedure for controlled delivery of the gas is as follows:

1. Turn the delivery pressure adjusting screw anticlockwise until it rotates freely. The regulator is then closed.

2. Open the cylinder valve by slowly turning the spindle anticlockwise with the recommended key, until the cylinder pressure gauge shows the tank pressure. Do not open the valve any further.

3. Close the output needle valve.

4. Turn the delivery pressure adjusting screw clockwise until the required output pressure (typically 10psi) is registered on the outlet pressure gauge.

5. When the gas line is correctly attached to the apparatus (see Section 6.2) open the needle valve slowly to obtain the desired flow rate.

When the gas is no longer required the flow should be shut off and the cylinder closed by closing the regulator (rotate the pressure adjusting screw anticlockwise) and then closing the cylinder valve. The cylinder valve should always be shut when the gas is not in use.

Lecture bottles should also be fitted with a regulator and needle valve, as specified by the manufacturer. The regulators are of two types, one for corrosive and one for non-corrosive gases, and they require a Teflon or lead washer. The procedures for using lecture bottles are the same as for larger cylinders.

A number of gases are supplied in liquefied form at relatively low pressures and these generally only require the use of a flow control valve. The valves on these cylinders are generally fitted with a handwheel. Again you should consult the supplier's technical data for information on the correct fittings and handling procedures.

6.3   Handling gases

This section is concerned with general procedures for handling gases and includes a discussion of apparatus and techniques for adding them to reaction flasks,. The preparation and scrubbing of some common reagent gases are described in Section 6.6. Methods for use of inert gases to protect air sensitive reactions are detailed in Chapter 8. Hydrogenation, ozonolysis, and liquid ammonia reactions are described in Chapter 14.

Two important principles must be borne in mind when carrying out a reaction involving a gas.

1. A pressure release device, such as an oil or mercury bubbler, must be attached to the apparatus in order to prevent the possibility of a dangerous pressure build-up.

2. Pressure fluctuations may result in the reaction mixture being sucked out of the reaction flask, so valves or traps must be placed in the gas line.

Reactions involving toxic gases must be carried out in an efficient fume hood.

A typical arrangement for the addition of a gas to a reaction flask is shown in Fig. 6.3. The gas is supplied from a cylinder or is prepared in another vessel and is supplied at a steady flow rate. It passes through an appropriately sized trap, such as a Dreschel bottle or an empty bubbler, before reaching the reaction flask. If a pressure reversal occurred and the contents of the flask were sucked back, the trap would prevent them from

Figure 6.3

coming into contact with the cylinder or the reagents used to prepare the gas. The gas can be bubbled into the solution *via* a needle or *via* a glass tube fitted with a wide bore glass frit. Use of a frit gives better dispersion of the gas but care should be taken that the frit does not become blocked by a solid product.

It is important to place an oil or mercury bubbler between the gas supply and the trap so that if the gas line is blocked the gas can be vented safely. Obviously the depth of oil or mercury in the bubbler must be large enough to ensure that the gas will pass through the reaction mixture rather than venting from the bubbler. With the inclusion of a bubbler as a safety device, it is advisable to put clips on all the ground glass joints, or to wrap them securely with Teflon tape, so that the gas cannot leak from the apparatus.

The type of tubing used in the line will be dictated by the nature of the gas. Rubber or PVC tubing is convenient for non-corrosive, non-toxic gases such as carbon dioxide but many reagent gases require the use of glass or resistant plastic tubing. A brief guide to the chemical resistance of some common tubing materials is provided below, and more detailed information about specific products can be obtained from manufacturers. Caution should be exercized when corrosive and toxic gases are used.

PVC (Tygon)

Flexible with low permeability but poor resistance to organic solvents and acidic gases.

Polyethylene, polypropylene

Better resistance to solvents and acids than PVC but not suitable for halogens.

Fluorocarbons (Teflon)

Poor flexibility, but excellent chemical resistance.

Natural rubber

High gas permeability and low chemical resistance.

Neoprene

Relatively good resistance to organic solvents and to acids.

Fluorocarbon rubber (Viton)

Expensive but good chemical resistance. Unsuitable for amines and ammonia.

Gas which is not absorbed can escape *via* a bubbler. Small quantities of non-toxic gases can be allowed to vent into an efficient fume-cupboard. Toxic gases should be passed through a scrubbing system and suitable procedures for various gases are described in Section 6.6. The bubbler also provides a means of monitoring the rate of uptake of the gas, and the flow rate should be adjusted so that very little is vented. For relatively insoluble gases, or for slow reactions, it may be necessary to stir or shake the reaction flask.

6.4 Measurement of gases

The addition of an accurately measured quantity of a gas is sometimes necessary, for example to obtain selective hydrogenation of a diene. Some convenient and reasonably accurate methods for measuring gases are described in this section.

Use of standardized solutions

If a gas is soluble in a suitable solvent, and the concentration of the solution can be determined by a simple analytical technique, then accurately measured quantities of the gas can be dispensed by using the appropriate volume of the solution. For example solutions of the hydrogen halides in various solvents can be determined by simple acid/base titration and solutions of chlorine in carbon tetrachloride can be determined by addition of excess potassium iodide and back titration with sodium thiosulphate. Refer to textbooks of inorganic analysis for details of these methods.

Using gas-tight syringes

Commercially available gas-tight syringes provide the most convenient method for dispensing small volumes of gases. A syringe fitted with an on/off valve and a needle (Fig. 6.4) is repeatedly filled with the gas and then emptied again, to remove the air. It is then filled to the required volume from a gas stream, pressurized by a bubbler, and the valve is shut.

gas-tight
syringe

valve with
Luer-lock
fittings

inert
gas line

Figure 6.4

Just before use, the valve is opened to purge the needle and allow the gas to reach atmospheric pressure, and then the needle is inserted into the reaction flask. If a small volume of gas is involved (less than 100ml) the reaction vessel can be a sealed system and the gas can be added slowly from the syringe. For larger volumes the reaction flask should be fitted with a mercury bubbler and the gas should be added at such a rate that gas does not vent from the bubbler.

Using a gas burette

Gas burettes are most commonly used for low pressure hydrogenations, but they can of course be used for delivering other gases thus providing an easy method of dispensing accurately measured volumes. A simple gas burette design is shown in Fig. 6.5. It is operated as follows:

1. Open the double oblique tap to the vent (fume hood), and the three-way tap to the burette. Raise the levelling bulb to expel most of the gas from the burette.
2. Turn the double oblique tap to the gas line, turn on the gas supply, and fill the burette slowly, lowering the levelling bulb as the burette fills.
3. Repeat steps 1 and 2 twice more to ensure that all of the air has been expelled. Then fill the burette to approximately 20% more than the required volume.
4. Open the three-way tap to the line fitted with a needle, which can be inserted into the reaction flask, and flush the tubing with gas. Turn off the gas supply.

Figure 6.5

5. Open the three-way tap to connect the burette to the line with the needle, thus allowing the gas to come to atmospheric pressure and giving the the needle a final flush. Rapidly read the volume in the burette and insert the needle into the reaction flask.

6. Raise the levelling bulb slowly to keep a slight positive pressure of the gas as the reaction proceeds. When the required volume has been added, close the three-way tap. If the gas is hazardous flush the apparatus with inert gas (steps 1-4) after use.

If gas burettes are used for a variety of different gases then some safety points should be noted. The burette should be thoroughly flushed with inert gas after each use. The tubing may need to be changed for use with different gases, and the liquid in the reservoir may also need to be changed depending on the application (aqueous copper sulphate, mercury, mineral oil, and dibutyl phthalate are often used). The gas burette method is particularly good for reactions in which the uptake of gas is slow. Gas burettes are also used for measuring the volume of gas absorbed, or evolved, in a reaction. A useful application is the quantitative analysis of hydride solutions by adding the hydride to an excess of protic or acidic solvent, and measuring the volume of hydrogen evolved.[3]

The procedure for the analysis of $BH_3.THF$ is illustrative.

1. Place 50 ml of a 1:1 mixture of glycerol and water, and a stirring bar, in a flask and seal it with a rubber septum. Connect to the gas burette using a needle as before.

2. Open the burette to the flask and add a few millilitres of hydride solution to the flask in order to saturate the atmosphere with hydrogen.

3. Open the burette to the atmosphere and raise the levelling bulb to give a reading of approximately zero. Note this reading.

4. Turn the three-way tap so that the burette is connected only to the flask. Add an accurately measured volume of hydride solution, with rapid stirring. The volume used should be sufficient to more than half fill the gas burette you are using.

5. When hydrogen evolution has ceased, lower the levelling bulb so that the liquid levels in the burette and the reservoir are equal, and read the volume. Calculate the molarity using the following equation.

3. H.C. Brown, *Organic Synthesis via Boranes*, Wiley, New York, 1975.

Molarity $=\dfrac{(P_a-P_s)(273)(V_h-V_a)}{((760)(T)(22.4)(V_a)}$

P_a = Atmospheric pressure (mmHg)

P_s = Vapour pressure of the solvent in the resevoir at temp. T (mmHg)

V_h = Volume of hydrogen evolved (ml)

V_a = Volume of hydride solution added (ml)

T = Temperature (°K)

This method should give an accuracy of better than ±5%.

6. Repeat the measurements until reproducible results are obtained.

By condensing the gas

Many gases (see Appendix 2) have relatively high boiling points so they can easily be liquefied and measured in the liquid form. The gas is passed into a vessel, which is then cooled to the appropriate temperature, as shown in Fig. 6.6. The quantity of condensed gas can be measured by

Figure 6.6

volume or by weight. When the required quantity has been condensed the cylinder is closed and the reaction flask is attached to the safety trap. The cooling bath is then removed and the gas allowed to distil into the reaction vessel. The mercury bubbler and safety trap serve the usual functions.

Using a quantitative reaction

A specific quantity of gas can be added to a reaction if the gas is prepared using a chemical reaction of known yield. Methods and apparatus for preparing some commonly used gases are described in Section 6.6 and mention must also be made of an elegant gas generator devised by H.C. Brown, which is described in detail elsewhere.[3]

6.5   Inert gases

Nitrogen and argon are by far the most commonly used inert gases and techniques for conducting reactions under an inert atmosphere are described in Chapter 8. Both N_2 and Ar are available in various grades of purity and usually gas of 99.995% purity can be used without further purification. Attempted purification using conventional drying trains is generally counter-productive. An easy method of checking whether your inert gas line is absolutely dry is to place a flask containing some titanium tetrachloride on the manifold. Evacuate carefully for a few seconds and then open to the inert gas. If you see white fumes of titanium dioxide, you have a poor batch of gas or a leak in your gas line. Effective gas purification systems are described elsewhere.[4,5] Although it is more expensive, argon is superior to nitrogen in two important respects. It is heavier than air and therefore protects the contents of a flask more effectively, and it is completely inert whereas nitrogen does react with some materials, the most commonly encountered examples being lithium metal and some transition metal complexes.

6.6   Reagent gases

It may occasionally be necessary to prepare a gas, if a cylinder is not available. Methods for the preparation (and scrubbing) of some simple gases are provided in this section. Most of these preparations can be carried out in the apparatus shown in Fig. 6.7.

Figure 6.7

The solution in the pressure-equalizing dropping funnel is added *slowly and cautiously* to the reagent in the flask, with stirring and cooling if necessary. The gas then passes through a suck-back trap and on to the reaction flask, and any that is not absorbed passes through a scrubber. As usual, there are two bubblers, the first to prevent pressure build-up and the second to monitor the amount of gas which is not being absorbed. The rate of addition of the reagents should be adjusted so that relatively little of the gas escapes through the second bubbler. This bubbler also provides a gas-tight seal to the atmosphere which protects the reaction flask from the reagent (often water) used in the scrubber. If a toxic gas is being generated, the apparatus should be flushed with an inert gas before dismantling.

4.   D.F. Shriver and M.A. Drezdzon, *The Manipulation of Air-Sensitive Compounds,* 2nd ed., Wiley, New York, 1986.

5.   A.L. Wayda and M.Y. Darensbourg Eds., *Experimental Organometallic Chemistry, A Practicum in Synthesis and Characterization,* American Chemical Society, Washington, 1987.

Various types of scrubber may be employed but the simplest method of scrubbing relatively small quantities of water-soluble gases is to pass them through water. Two simple devices for this purpose are shown below. The first (Fig. 6.8(a)) is suitable only for small quantities of gas whereas the second (Fig. 6.8(b)) is more appropriate for larger volumes.

(a)   (b)

Figure 6.8

Methods for preparing some common gases are described below (see ref. 3 for other methods). The properties of these and other gases are listed in Appendix 2. Many of these gases are very harmful and they should only be handled in an efficient fume cupboard, taking care to prevent leaks and to scrub any excess gas.

Acetylene

Prepare by addition of water to calcium carbide and dry by passing through a column of molecular sieves. Acetylene can explode spontaneously, especially when pressurized. For this reason the gas should be generated very cautiously, the generator should be cooled, and the gas line should be fitted with a bubbler so that the pressure cannot rise above 15 psi. Dispose by venting slowly in an efficient hood.

Carbon dioxide

The simplest method is to allow solid carbon dioxide to evaporate, and the gas can be dried by passage over molecular sieves. It can also be prepared by addition of dilute hydrochloric acid to calcium carbonate. Passage over molecular sieves will remove any aqueous acid in the gas stream.

Carbon monoxide

Carbon monoxide is very toxic by inhalation: TLV 50ppm. Prepare by slow addition of anhydrous formic acid to concentrated sulphuric acid at 90-100°C (frothing tends to be a problem). One millilitre of formic acid generates 26.6 mmoles of gas. The CO is contaminated with small amounts of carbon dioxide and sulphur dioxide which may be removed by passage over potassium hydroxide or the commercial product Ascarite (sodium hydroxide on silica). Dispose of carbon monoxide by slow venting in an efficient hood.

Chlorine

Chlorine is extremely toxic and a powerful irritant: TLV 1ppm. Prepare by slow addition of concentrated hydrochloric acid to potassium permanganate (6.2ml of acid per gram of permanganate), with occasional shaking. The gas evolution slows as the reaction proceeds and warming is required to complete the reaction; 1.12g of chlorine should be formed per gram of permanganate but in our experience the yield is substantially lower than this. Chlorine may be stored in solution in carbon tetrachloride. Dispose by dissolving in water.

Diazomethane

See Chapter 5.

Hydrogen bromide

HBr is corrosive and toxic: TLV 3ppm. It can be prepared by slow addition of bromine to purified tetralin, with stirring. The small amount of bromine which passes over with the HBr can be removed by passing the gas through a trap containing pure dry tetralin. Dispose by dissolving in water.

Hydrogen chloride

Hydrogen chloride is corrosive and toxic: TLV 5ppm. Prepare by adding concentrated sulphuric acid to anhydrous ammonium chloride and dry by passage over molecular sieves. Dispose by dissolving in water.

CHAPTER 7

Vacuum Pumps

7.1 Introduction

There are a variety of tasks in organic chemistry which require provision of a vacuum source. However, different tasks will require different levels of vacuum and more than one type of vacuum source will be needed to service all the requirements of the lab. We can split vacuum supplies loosely into two categories: low vacuum, being 1-50mmHg and high vacuum being below 1mmHg. A low vacuum source is valuable for such tasks as vacuum filtration, operation of rotary evaporators and vacuum distillation of relatively volatile liquids. High vacuum is required for serving inert gas line manifolds, vacuum distillations and drying solids by removing traces of solvent or moisture from them.

7.2 Low vacuum pumps

7.2.1 Water aspirators

The water aspirator is probably the most common laboratory vacuum source. It is normally possible to achieve a vacuum of about 10-12mmHg using a normal cold water supply, and this is adequate for many requirements. The advantage of the water aspirator is that it is cheap, simple to operate and fairly reliable. Its main disadvantage is that it is prone to 'suck-back', which can leave your apparatus full of water! This occurs if the water pressure drops after a good vacuum has built up in the apparatus. The same thing will happen if the tap is turned off while the system is still under vacuum. For this reason the tap should always be kept full on, and an air inlet should be provided by means of a 3-way tap. A simple trap should also be incorporated, which will give you some time to disconnect the apparatus if suck-back occurs (Fig. 7.1). A water trap will not prevent suck-back altogether and hence it is not advisable to leave apparatus unattended while connected to an aspirator. Clearly, this type of pump is not suitable for connecting to an inert gas manifold.

Figure 7.1

Other disadvantages of the water aspirator are that it is quite noisy and uses a considerable volume of water if it is left on for prolonged periods.

7.2.2 House vacuum systems

Many large laboratory buildings have a large central vacuum pump which serves a house vacuum system. There are great variations in the effectiveness of such systems, depending on the type of pump employed, the number of users and various other factors. A good house vacuum system will pull about 50mmHg and can be very useful for driving rotary evaporators, filtrations and simple vacuum distillations. The advantage of the system is ease of use, but the vacuum can fluctuate quite considerably depending on how many people are using it.

7.2.3 Electric diaphragm pumps

There are now a number of simple low-vacuum electric pumps available that will produce a vacuum of about 12mmHg. Some of these pumps are specially designed to withstand solvent vapours and are therefore suitable for use with rotary evaporators. They are clearly an alternative to water pumps and, although the initial capital expenditure is much higher, they have several advantages: they are quiet, there are no problems of 'suck-back' and they do   not use vast quantities of water.

For some tasks very cheap and simple fishtank-type diaphragm pumps are useful. These will produce a vacuum of about 300mmHg and can also be used to provide compressed air for pressurizing chromatography columns (see Chapter 9).

7.3 High vacuum pumps

7.3.1 Rotary oil pumps

Rotary oil pumps will provide a reliable vacuum down to about 0.01mmHg (at the apparatus) and are thus one of the most valuable pieces of equipment in the lab, being used for a wide variety of tasks. Ideally every research worker should have his/her own high vacuum pump, but in many cases cost prohibits this and pumps are shared. If a pump is shared, it is common to have it mounted on a trolley which has all the ancillary devices (traps, gauge etc.) mounted on it. Alternatively, a shared pump may be fixed in one place, but attached to a communal manifold, distillation set-up or other piece of apparatus. A good two-stage pump is suitable for most high vacuum requirements in an organic chemistry lab.

Solvent traps

A high vacuum pump must be fitted with efficient solvent traps to prevent the pump oil from becoming contaminated. The traps are simply cold finger condensers incorporated into the vacuum line before it enters the pump. It is preferable to have two traps which can be cooled by either liquid nitrogen, or solid CO_2-acetone, but if only one trap is used solid CO_2-acetone will be ineffective and liquid nitrogen must be used as the coolant. A typical design for a trapping system is given in Fig. 7.2.

If the trapping system incorporates a cone joint, it can be connected directly to a manifold such as that shown in Fig. 3.1 (Chapter 3). Alternatively, a piece of high vacuum tubing can be used to connect the traps to a distillation apparatus, a double manifold (Fig. 3.4, Chapter 3), or any other piece of equipment.

Figure 7.2

Operating a high vacuum pump

Do not immerse the traps in liquid nitrogen unless they are evacuated, as this will cause liquid air to condense. The result of this can be a violent explosion, caused by re-vaporization or by oxidations of organic solvents etc.

Before switching the pump on check that the traps are empty. Then with the 2-way tap closed and the 3-way tap open between the pump and the traps, but closed to the vent, turn the pump on. Next immerse the traps in Dewars filled with liquid nitrogen and check the vacuum by connecting a vacuum gauge to the 3-way tap. If the vacuum is satisfactory (<1mm), the 2-way tap can be opened, to evacuate the apparatus which is connected to it. The vacuum should then be checked again to make sure there are no leaks in the system.

When you want to switch the pump off, close the 2-way tap, turn the 3-way tap to vent through the pump (*not into the traps*), then turn the pump off. Remove the liquid nitrogen Dewars from the traps immediately after switching the pump off and then vent air into the traps using the 3-way tap. It is very important to vent the pump before turning it off otherwise pump oil may suck back into the traps.

Care of high vacuum pumps

High vacuum pumps are very expensive items, but they will give very reliable service for many years if they are treated properly. For an organic chemist to work efficiently he/she must be able to rely on pumps working properly and this will only be the case if they are treated with care. The main reason for deterioration of vacuum pumps is contamination of the oil with volatile organic compounds and acidic vapours such as HCl or HBr. To avoid this problem, you should be very conscientious about keeping the coolant well topped-up around the traps, and emptying them regularly. No matter how careful you are, some solvent vapour will always find its way into the pump, and for this reason the oil should be changed regularly, at least once a month for a pump which is used every day.

7.3.2 Vapour diffusion pumps

Occasionally a distillation will require a higher vacuum than that produced by a rotary pump. Higher vacuums are normally obtained by employing a mercury or oil vapour diffusion pump, in conjunction with a rotary pump. Oil vapour pumps are most commonly used today and various models are now commercially available which will produce a vacuum of about 10^{-5}mmHg. These pumps are only used occasionally but it is very useful to have one shared between a large group or section.

7.4   Pressure measurement and regulation

It is very important to be able to measure the pressure in a vacuum system, particularly when carrying out a distillation. For low vacuum measurement a simple manometer, such as that shown in Fig. 7.3a, is commonly used and the pressure is taken by subtracting the heights of the mercury levels. Dial gauges are also useful for in-line measurements and they are particularly valuable when used with rotary evaporators. For high vacuum measurement a McLeod gauge, with a range of 1 to 0.001mmHg, is most commonly used (Fig. 7.3b). The gauge is rotated into the vertical position to read the vacuum, but must be turned back to the horizontal position and back again to vertical, in order to read a change in pressure. Electronic Pirani gauges are also available for measuring high vacuum.

Quite a common requirement is for a distillation pressure somewhat higher than that delivered by the high vacuum pump. Achieving this is no simple matter because a very accurate leak must be provided in order to maintain a constant vacuum. There are various devices available, one of the simplest being an accurate needle valve (such as an Edwards LV5) which will be suitable for most distillation purposes.

Figure 7.3

7.4.1 Units of pressure (vacuum) measurement

There is often confusion about different units of pressure measurement, but the way they relate to one another is quite simple. The most common units are mm Hg, and 1mm Hg is the same as 1Torr. The other common scale is mbar which relates to atmospheric pressure, 1 bar = 1 atmosphere = 760mm. Thus:

$$1mbar = 0.76mmHg = 0.76Torr$$

CHAPTER 8

Carrying Out The Reaction

8.1 Introduction

This is the most important single chapter in this book. In order to be certain of the results of a particular experiment, and to ensure reproducibility, it is important that the appropriate precautions are taken, and that proper preparations are made. Many common organic reactions involve the use of air sensitive reagents, which requires the reaction to be carried out under inert, anhydrous conditions. These conditions are also used for reactions which are sensitive to the presence of water. Indeed the majority of reactions, although not requiring such conditions, will usually benefit from being carried out in the absence of air and water. Accordingly most of this chapter is concerned with the use of air sensitive reagents, since the same basic techniques can be used for almost all types of reactions likely to be encountered.

First of all, before attempting the reaction it is important to ensure that you have the necessary glassware, apparatus, reagents, and experimental procedure (including work up and a tlc system which will allow you to follow the reaction). Do not forget to check on the safety aspects of the chemicals (including solvents), of the likely reaction products, and of the procedures which you will be using. As alluded to above, most reactions will require monitoring of some kind (tlc, gc, hplc, etc.) and it is important to ensure that your chosen system is suitable for the starting material, and give some consideration as to where the expected product is likely to be found (will the polarity increase or decrease on converting starting material to product?). Make certain that you allow yourself plenty of time to complete the reaction, or at least to monitor it in the early stages if it is likely to be a lengthy experiment. Finally it is most important that the reaction is written up carefully as you go along, rather than writing it up 'properly' a few days later for the reasons given in the section on keeping your laboratory notebook. Remember, it is important to write up experiments which have 'failed' as carefully as those which are successful. If this is done the reason for 'failure' might be apparent to you at a later stage, and in any case this detailed information is likely to be of real value to someone following up your work.

8.2 Reactions with air sensitive reagents

8.2.1 Introduction

Many commonly used organic reagents are extremely reactive towards water and/or oxygen. Some examples are: alkyllithium reagents, Grignard reagents, organoboranes, metal hydrides, organoaluminium compounds, cuprates, titanium tetrachloride, dry solvents, etc. Some of these reagents are available commercially and others are prepared *in situ*, in either case they are most conveniently handled in solution. Although extreme care must be taken to exclude air and moisture when using these reagents, you should find them easy to handle once you become familiar with some simple techniques. General procedures for handling air sensitive reagents are described in Chapter 5 and the appropriate parts of that chapter should be consulted in conjunction with this section.

8.2.2 Preparing to carry out a reaction under inert conditions

If you already have permanent inert gas lines in the lab as suggested in Chapter 3, then carrying out a reaction under inert conditions should be routine. However, it is very important that you do not expose the reaction to the atmosphere at any stage. The techniques for ensuring this become second nature once you gain experience; but forward planning is always essential so that everything is in the right place at the right time and under an inert atmosphere. Therefore, before you start think very carefully about how you intend to carry out each operation of your reaction sequence, and list the equipment you will need. All equipment needs to be dried and cooled in advance and it is particularly important to have enough syringes available. Indeed, you should always have some spare dry syringes in case one gets jammed, contaminated or broken.

8.2.3 Drying and assembling glassware

It is assumed that the glassware has been cleaned before use and it is also important to check glassware, particularly flasks, for cracks and scratches especially if the glassware is going to be evacuated. If you are in doubt as to the safety of a particular item of glassware do not use it, and do not forget to get it repaired by the glassblower or to dispose of it. Do not leave it around for someone else to discover its weakness. Under normal conditions glassware has a thin film of water adsorbed to its surfaces which must be removed before moisture-sensitive reagents, dried solvents, or starting materials are allowed to come into contact with it. There are two basic methods for doing this. The first method is to heat the glassware in an oven at a temperature above 125°C for at least 6h, then quickly assemble it whilst hot and cool under a stream of dry inert gas. The second method is to assemble the glassware, evacuate it by connecting it to a double manifold/high vacuum pump, then heat the whole set-up with either a bunsen or heat-gun. The two-way tap on the manifold is then switched so that the apparatus filled with argon (or nitrogen) while it cools, leaving the apparatus set up and ready for use. This procedure can save a good deal of time but, *because of the dangers involved in heating glassware under vacuum, this procedure is best reserved for small-scale reactions.*

Glassware and normal syringes can be dried in an oven then cooled in a desiccator over P_2O_5 or self-indicating silica gel, but it is not advisable to heat microlitre syringes and these should be dried under vacuum in a desiccator.

If you are going to use magnetic stirring, do not forget to include a stirrer bar before the apparatus is assembled and before the drying procedure is carried out, since the stirrer bar will also be covered in a film of moisture and adding it later is likely to introduce air and moisture into the system.

It is not advisable to use grease for glassware assembly, since this will eventually find its way into your reaction product. If you have to use it, always use the minimum quantity possible and remove it carefully from the joint immediately after the reaction has been quenched. This can be done using a tissue dampened with chloroform or other halogenated solvent. It is important to do this before addition of an extraction solvent, or before pouring the reaction mixture through the joint. Rather than use grease, it is much better to use Teflon tape or sleeves, since these are at least as efficient, do not contaminate your product, and in the case of sleeves they are reusable. It is also advisable to seal the outside of the joint by wrapping Teflon tape around to cover the 'join'. This will help to prevent any condensation on the outside of the glassware from finding its way into the reaction. Joint clips (e.g. Bibby clips) should be used on all accessible joints.

8.2.4 Typical reaction set-ups using a double manifold

A double manifold (Fig. 8.1) is an extremely useful piece of apparatus, especially for carrying out reactions under inert atmosphere and its installation is described in more detail in Chapter 3. One barrel of the manifold is connected to a high vacuum pump (or house vacuum system) and another to a cylinder of dry inert gas. Its main advantage is that, simply by turning the two-way tap on one of the outlets, any vessel connected to that outlet can be switched instantaneously from vacuum to inert gas atmosphere or *vice versa*. Several reactions can also be set up at once, the only limit being the number of outlets. At the end of the argon (or nitrogen) line there is a bubbler which prevents air from being sucked back into the system, and provides a convenient means of monitoring the gas flow rate.

Figure 8.1

A fast flow is used when filling a system, but once the reaction is set up, one bubble every 5-10s is adequate. A piece of apparatus which is very useful when used in conjunction with a double manifold is a Quickfit 3-way tap, which is also described in more detail in Chapter 3.

8.2.5 Basic procedure for inert atmosphere reactions

A typical simple reaction set-up using a manifold is shown in Fig. 8.1 and the following general procedure is applicable to a wide range of reactions. However, this is only intended to be a general guide-line and can easily be modified to suit various requirements. Some of these modifications are discussed later in this chapter.

Before starting decide on the order for addition of reagents and if possible arrange this so that any solid reagent is added first. If this is not possible try to add the solid as a solution, using the technique described later. If a reagent really does have to be added as a solid, this can be done successfully and again a method will be described to do this.

Make sure before you start that you have all the *dry* syringes, needles, and any other ancillary items, and that you are familiar with the operation of the manifold and the 3-way Quickfit tap.

1. *Set up and dry the system*

   Connect the reaction flask *including stirrer bar* to the manifold (Fig. 8.1), set the 2-way tap on the manifold and the 3-way tap on the reaction flask (position A, Fig. 8.2a) so that the system is evacuated, and heat the glassware with a heat gun (or bunsen) for 5min. Then,

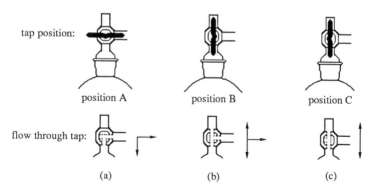

Figure 8.2 Flow through a 3-way tap relative to tap position.

with inert gas flowing through the bubbler at a rapid rate, turn the manifold tap *slowly* to introduce the inert gas. Keep an eye on the bubbler while you are switching to the inert gas supply and operate the tap carefully to avoid 'suck-back'. Finally leave the apparatus to cool.

2. *Add initial reactants*

Solid reactants (or heavy gum oils) can be weighed into the reaction flask at this stage. With the inert gas flow at a reasonably high level, remove the flask from the system and quickly weigh the reagent into it (for reactive solids see Chapter 5). Then re-attach the flask to the 3-way tap and switch the manifold tap to evacuate. If there are traces of solvent on the reactant these can be removed by leaving the flask under vacuum for an extended period, otherwise the 2-way tap can be switched back to argon straight away leaving the reactant in the flask under inert atmosphere.

3. *Add solvent*

The best way to add solvent to the system, and avoid breaking the inert atmosphere, is to use a syringe. It is best to syringe the solvent straight from the collecting head of a still, which is itself under inert atmosphere (see Chapter 4), but the solvent might also be taken from a bottle or flask under inert atmosphere (see Chapter 5). In either case, once you have a syringe loaded with solvent, open the 3-way tap to position B (Fig. 8.2b), keeping an inert gas flow *which is rapid enough to maintain bubbling*, and add the solvent. Then turn 3-way tap back to position A (Fig. 8.2a) and reduce gas pressure to maintain steady bubbling. For large scale reactions solvents can be added by disconnecting the flask, adding the solvent quickly and re-assembling, but this inevitably leads to air entering the system. With higher boiling solvents the air can be removed by sequentially partially evacuating and refilling with inert gas several times, using the 2-way manifold tap.

4. *Cool the flask*

At this stage the reaction flask can be immersed in a cooling bath and stirred with a magnetic stirrer (see Chapter 8). *Never cool a flask before it is under the inert atmosphere as this causes moisture to condense.*

Figure 8.3

5. *Add reagents*

It is most commonly the reagents used in the reaction which are air and/or moisture sensitive and they should be added with great care (see Chapter 5 for more detail). After pressurizing the reagent container with inert gas, syringe out the required quantity (Fig. 8.3a). Increase the inert gas flow through the manifold so that rapid bubbling is maintained as the 3-way tap is opened to position B, then insert the syringe through the tap to deliver the reagent (Fig. 8.3b). When all the reagent has been added turn the 3-way tap back to position A and reduce the gas flow so that there is a bubble every few seconds (Fig. 8.3c). Any further reagents are added in the same way and the reaction is left to proceed. To add a cooled reagent it is advisable to use a cannula made out of Teflon tubing (see Chapter 5, Section 5.4.3 for more detail).

6. *Reaction monitoring*

The reaction can easily be monitored by tlc, gc, etc. Again increase the inert gas flow through the manifold so that rapid bubbling is maintained as the 3-way tap is opened to position B, then insert a drawn piece of glass tubing or Pasteur pipette through the tap to remove a drop of the mixture.

7. *Work-up*

Once the reaction is complete it can be worked up as normal (see Chapter 9). However, when there is the likelihood of residual reactive reagents such as organometallics, be very careful when adding aqueous solutions It is normally safer to keep the mixture under an inert atmosphere whilst the solution is added.

8.2.6 *Modifications to basic procedure*

1. *Reactions at elevated temperatures*

When a reaction needs to be heated or when there is any possibility that it might be exothermic, a condenser should be incorporated into the reaction set-up. Normal Liebig condensers have the water jacket next to the outer surface and there is always the possibility of atmospheric moisture condensing on the outside, running down to the ground glass joint, and seeping into the reaction flask. Teflon sleeved joints should prevent water getting into the reaction vessel, but a better method is to use coil type-

Figure 8.4

condensers (Fig. 8.4) for reactions under inert conditions. Since the cooling surfaces are inside the apparatus, the problem of outside condensation is alleviated.

Typical set-ups for reactions which are to be heated are shown in Fig. 8.4. The procedure for carrying out the reaction is exactly as described in the previous section, except that the reaction is heated instead of being cooled. Reagents can be added through the 3-way tap, provided a syringe with a long needle is used, or as an alternative a flask with a side arm fitted with a septum can be used. *Whilst the temperature of a reaction is changing the bubbler of the system should be checked to make sure there is a constant inert gas pressure.*

2. Slow addition of reagents and large scale work

When slow addition of an air-sensitive reagent is required it is best to incorporate a pressure equalizing addition funnel into the apparatus, and for

Figure 8.5

large scale work this is always best. The apparatus can be set up with or without a condenser, can be stirred either magnetically or mechanically. A typical arrangement is shown in Fig. 8.5. Where very careful slow addition is required, particular on a small scale, the use of a syringe pump is strongly advised. These are mechanical devices which drive the plunger of a syringe very slowly into the barrel.

(a) Cooling apparatus under inert atmosphere

(b) Filling dropping funnel using cannula

Figure 8.6

To dry this larger, more elaborate set-up, it is best to oven-dry the equipment first, assemble it hot and leave to cool under a stream of inert gas. This can be done by connecting to inert gas from the manifold, with a short needle through the septum acting as a vent (Fig. 8.6a). Once the apparatus is cool reactants can be added as described above. A syringe can be used to add small quantities of reagent to the addition funnel. For larger quantities (>50ml) the cannulation technique described in Chapter 5 for bulk transfer of liquids is best, and if the funnel is graduated the reagent can be added straight from the reagent bottle (Fig. 8.6b). If a mechanical stirrer is used a Teflon sealed guide should be used for the stirrer rod. The reaction is carried out exactly as before.

3. Addition of a reagent prepared separately, or of a solid

reaction flask ⟶   ⟵ reagent

Figure 8.7

When a solid reagent is to be added to a reaction set-up which is already under inert conditions, it is best to add it in solution. To do this, weigh the solid into a dry flask, fit the flask with a 3-way tap, connect to a separate outlet on the manifold, and evacuate. Then switch the manifold tap to introduce inert gas, and with the gas flow high enough to maintain rapid bubbling at the bubbler, open the 3-way tap to position B and syringe in the required dry solvent. With the 3-way tap turned back to position A, the solution is under inert atmosphere and can be kept indefinitely (Fig. 8.7). To transfer the reagent, make sure that the inert gas flow is high enough to maintain rapid bubbling whilst the 3-way tap on the reagent vessel is opened to position B. Then syringe out the solution, turn the tap back to position A, open the tap on the reaction flask to position B and add the reagent. Alternatively, a cannula can be used to transfer the reagent (see below).

A similar procedure can be used when a reagent has to be prepared under inert conditions for use in the reaction. This is quite a common occurrence, for example when a Grignard or alkyllithium reagent has to be prepared, then added to a reaction mixture. In this case the reaction flask assembly is set up attached to one outlet of the manifold, while the reagent is prepared in an appropriate set-up at another outlet. The reagent can easily be transferred to the reaction flask using a syringe.

For large scale transfers, or for the transfer of a pre-cooled solution, a cannula can be used. To use a cannula, first fit the 3-way tap of the reagent flask with a septum, turn the tap to the closed position and disconnect from

(a)   (b)

Figure 8.8

the manifold. Then pressurize the flask with a separate inert gas supply, turn the 3-way tap to position B, insert a cannula, and transfer the solution either to the reaction flask directly (Fig. 8.8a), or to an addition funnel (Fig. 8.8b).

For more information about cannulation and adjustment of inert gas pressures see Chapter 5, Section 5.4.2.

4. Direct addition of a solid to a reaction under inert atmosphere

Although it is much easier to add solids in solution, on some occasions a solid will have to be added directly. With the apparatus connected to a manifold and with argon as the inert gas, the procedure is often quite simple. A reaction flask with a stoppered side arm should be used and, after first increasing the argon flow to give very rapid bubbling, the stopper can be removed to add the solid reactant. If this procedure is used, great care should be taken. The stopper should be removed for the minimum time

Figure 8.9

required to add the reagent, and you should make sure that it is not added at a rate which might lead to the reaction going out of control. Alternatively, an inverted funnel (see Chapter 5) can be used to blanket the apparatus with an inert atmosphere to protect the reaction mixture.

There are alternative arrangements for adding solids, but none are universal. One method is to attach a bent tube containing the solid to the side arm of the flask, and twist the tube to allow the compound to pour into the reaction flask (Fig. 8.9).

8.2.7 Use of balloons for holding an inert atmosphere

Although we recommend using the double manifold techniques described above, reactions can also be kept under inert atmosphere by using a balloon filled with inert gas (Fig. 8.10). This can prove particularily useful if a double manifold system is not available. To do this you first fill the balloon

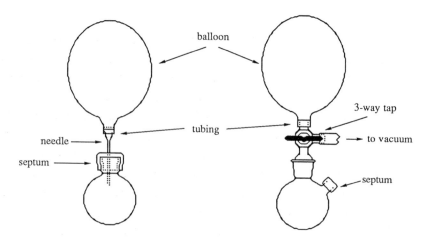

Figure 8.10

with the inert gas from a cylinder, then attach it to the reaction system using either a needle/septum or 3-way tap, taking care to ensure that there are no leaks in the system.

In the case of the needle/septum attachment, any air contained in the reaction flask is then flushed out by using another needle to vent the system (Fig. 8.11). After the reaction flask has been thoroughly flushed with the inert gas, the extra needle is removed and the reaction flask is ready for use. The balloon keeps the whole system under a positive pressure of the inert gas, and also allows liquid materials to be added to, or removed from, the flask *via* syringe insertion through the septum.

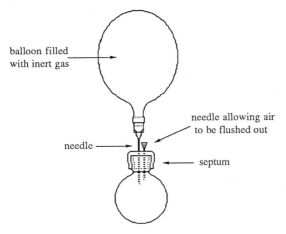

balloon filled with inert gas

needle allowing air to be flushed out

needle

septum

Figure 8.11

Generally argon is preferred when using this technique because it is more dense than air, and will fill the reaction flask, pushing out any air more effectively than would nitrogen. This technique can also be employed when syringing air-sensitive materials from bottles or containers.

With the three-way tap attachment, a vacuum line can be connected (Fig. 8.10). The system can then be purged by sequentially evacuating, then filling with the inert gas from the balloon. This is a more effective procedure than simply flushing out the flask and so both nitrogen and argon can be used with this set-up. Liquid materials can then be added to the flask by syringe *via* the septum inlet as before.

Since balloons are perishable it is often advisable to use a 'double balloon system'. This is simply two balloons, one inside the other, allowing the inert atmosphere to be maintained even if one bursts.

How to make a balloon attachment

Balloon attachments are easily constructed as outlined in Fig. 8.12. First the balloon (or double balloon) is pushed over a piece of rubber tubing which is about the same diameter as the balloon neck. This is secured in

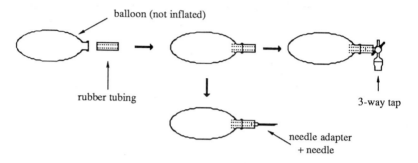

Figure 8.12

place using a piece of wire, elastic band, or parafilm. The open end of the tubing can then be attached to a three-way tap, or to a needle-tubing adapter and needle as shown. It is advisable to seal all joins with parafilm in order to ensure that there are no leaks.

Setting up a reaction

Once the balloon system has been constructed, the reaction system is simply set up as outlined in Fig. 8.10.

If the reaction is to be heated, a condenser will need to be fitted, in this case it may be necessary to use a two necked flask so that materials can be added to the flask. In such cases the balloon should be placed at the top of the condenser in order to prevent volatile liquids reaching it.

All joints should be sealed with Parafilm or Teflon tape, the latter being especially useful if the system is to be heated (Parafilm melts!).

8.2.8 The use of a 'spaghetti' tubing manifold

The main drawback with balloons is that they have a tendancy to burst and this can have grave consequences, especially if you are working on a small scale. A spaghetti manifold (Fig. 8.13) will provide a similar low pressure inert gas source, but is much more reliable. It is particularly useful if you need to set up several small scale reactions running in parallel to one another. This is often the case if you need to optimize the conditions for a reaction.

Figure 8.13

The reaction is set up in exactly the same way as described in the previous section for use of balloons. With either type of set-up a tlc sample can easily be removed by pushing a syringe needle through the septum then inserting the tlc capillary through it. When using the 'spaghetti' manifold it is often convenient to add reagents, or transfer them, by cannulation using a Teflon cannula (Fig. 8.14, see also Chapter 5, Section 5.4.2).

Figure 8.14

8.3   Reaction monitoring

Most people who are new recruits to the research labs learned their basic skills for carrying out reactions in an undergraduate laboratory. Inevitably, most of the organic chemistry undertaken in these lab classes involves following 'recipes', which have been well tried and tested. Therefore the conditions and the time taken for the reactions to reach completion is well established, and work-up can be carried out after a preset time. Unfortunately, the idea that you can guess the time it takes for a reaction to reach completion is a very bad habit to carry over into a research environment.

Every reaction you carry out should be monitored, and one of the first things you should do before starting any reaction is to decide on a suitable method for monitoring its progress. Even if you are following a literature procedure, reaction monitoring is still essential and it will usually save you time as well as giving you confidence about what is happening. Carrying out a reaction without monitoring its progress is like trying to thread a needle with your eyes closed!

The simplest and most universal method of reaction monitoring is thin layer chromatography (tlc) and this will be discussed first of all, but it is not *always* the best or only method, and sometimes you may have to use a little ingenuity to find an appropriate reaction monitoring technique.

8.3.1 Thin layer chromatography (tlc)

Tlc is a simple, but extremely powerful analytical tool. However it may take a little time before your expertise reaches a consistently high level, since a certain amount of intuition is always involved in choosing the appropriate solvent system, spotting the correct amount of sample, etc. Once you have gained experience and confidence in the use of tlc, you will find it extremely useful for a variety of purposes.

The main uses of tlc

1.   Tlc is normally the simplest and quickest way to monitor a reaction and the reaction mixture should be chromatographed against starting materials (and a co-spot). This allows you to follow how the reaction is progressing, and to assess when is the best time to work it up. In all

cases a record of the tlc should be made in your lab book (see Chapter 2).

2. Tlc can be used to indicate the identity of a compound, by comparing the unknown sample with a known material. In general each substance is spotted separately and also together (co-spot). Caution should be applied as co-running on tlc is *not* definitive proof of identity. Of course, substances that do not co-run are definitely not the same.

3. Tlc usually gives a good indication of the purity of a substance. Diastereoisomers can usually (but not always), be distinguished.

4. For flash chromatography (see Chapter 9), tlc is first used to determine the solvent system and quantity of silica required, and secondly to monitor the column fractions.

Tlc plates

There are two main types of coating for tlc plates, silica and alumina. Silica plates are most commonly used, they are slightly acidic and are suitable for running a broad range of compounds. Most of the information in this section refers directly to silica plates, but the same principles apply when using alumina plates. Alumina plates are slightly basic and are quite commonly used when a basic compound will not run very well on silica.

The most common tlc plates have either a glass or plastic backing coated with a thin layer of silica, which contains a binding agent to keep it bonded to the backing. Although tlc plates can be home-made, most people prefer to use commercial ones as they give very consistent results. For analytical purposes plates with a 0.25mm layer of silica are normally used. They are available in a variety of sizes, although 5 x 20cm is probably the most convenient size. The chromatographs are run along the 5cm length, cut to an appropriate width. This normally gives adequate resolution, with a very short running time. Plastic backed plates are sometimes cheaper and can easily be cut into strips with scissors, but glass plates seem to give better resolution and can be heated more vigorously for visualization purposes.

To cut a glass tlc plate, place it face down on a clean piece of paper, hold a ruler firmly along the proposed cut and draw a *sharp* diamond glass cutter along the line *once only*. Then holding the plate with the forefinger and thumb of each hand, on either side of the score line snap the plate along the line. With practice, and a good glass cutter, you should be able to cut plates down to about 1.5cm without ever spoiling them.

The procedure for running a tlc

1. Cut a tlc plate which is 5cm long, and wide enough so that about 0.5cm can be left between each spot (obviously the width of the plate is dependant upon the number of spots to be run on it).

2. Make a tlc spotter by drawing out a Pasteur pipette or melting point tube to about 0.5mm using a micro burner. The spotter can be used many times provided you wash it with clean solvent in between runs.

3. If the substance to be analysed is not already in solution, take it up in a volatile solvent as a ca. 1-2% solution. A non-polar solvent is preferable but methylene chloride is often used as a universal solvent for tlc samples. Reaction mixture solutions can be diluted down if necessary, and with experience making samples to a reasonable strength becomes intuitive.

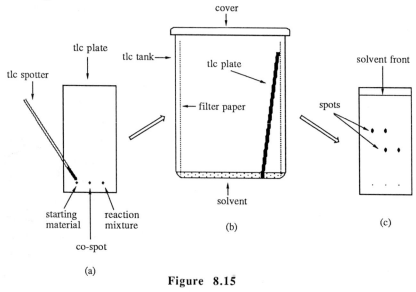

Figure 8.15

4. Using the spotter, spot a small amount of each solution about 0.5cm from the bottom of the plate, leaving a similar distance between each spot. The spots should be kept as small as possible, and you should take care to make sure that each of the spots is the same distance from the bottom of the plate (Fig. 8.15a).

The absolute distance which a compound runs up a tlc plate is extremely variable, depending on the exact conditions under which the plate was run. It is therefore much more informative to run comparative tlcs. When analysing a reaction mixture, it should always be run in comparison with the starting material and a mixed spot should also be run. This is very important because it often enables you to distinguish between compounds which run in almost identical positions.

5.   Place the plate upright in a tank lined with a filter paper and containing the chosen solvent system (to a depth of ca. 0.3cm as shown in Fig. 8.15b). Allow the solvent to creep up the tlc plate until it is ca. 0.3cm from the top, then remove it, and mark the level of the solvent front (Fig. 8.15c). A 150ml lipless beaker makes a convenient tlc tank and a petri dish can be used as a cover.

Detecting the spots

The three general ways to visualize spots on tlc plates are listed below. Any one or combination of these techniques can be used, but they should be carried out in the order shown, as the first two techniques are non-destructive.

1.   The plate can be viewed under a ultraviolet lamp to show any uv-active spots.

2.   The plate can be stained with iodine. This can be achieved rapidly, by shaking the plate in a bottle containing silica and a few crystals of iodine. The iodine will stain any compound that reacts with it and so is especially good for visualizing unsaturated compounds. Most spots show up within a few seconds, but the stain is not usually permanent.

3.   The plate can be treated with one of the reagents listed below and then heated to stain the spots. The reagent can be sprayed onto the plates, but this technique is quite hazardous and it is more effective for them to be dipped in the reagent. To do this, first let the tlc solvent evaporate, then holding the edge of the plate with tweezers, immerse the plate as completely as possible in the stain and remove it quickly. Rest the edge of the plate on a paper towel to absorb the excess stain before heating carefully on a hot plate or with a heat gun, until the spots show. This method is always permanent and so should be done last. When glass

plates are used the spots can sometimes be seen more clearly from the glass side of the plate.

Stains	Use/comments
Vanillin	Good general reagent, gives a range of colours.
PMA	Good general reagent, gives blue-green spots.
Anisaldehyde	Good general reagent, gives a range of colours.
Ceric sulphate	Fairly general, gives a range of colours.
DNP#	Mainly for aldehydes and ketones, gives orange spots.
Permanganate#	Mainly for unsaturated compounds and alcohols, gives yellow spots.

- usually do not require heating.

Recipes for visualization reagents.

Vanillin:	vanillin (15g) in ethanol (250ml) + conc. H_2SO_4 (2.5ml)
PMA:	phosphomolybdic acid (12g) in ethanol (250ml).
Anisaldehyde:	anisaldehyde (15g) in ethanol (250ml) + conc. H_2SO_4 (2.5ml).
Ceric sulphate:	15% aqueous H_2SO_4 saturated with ceric sulphate.
DNP:	2,4-dinitrophenolhydrazine (12g) + conc. H_2SO_4 (60ml) + water (80ml) + ethanol (200ml).
Permanganate:	$KMnO_4$ (3g) + K_2CO_3 (20g) + 5% aqueous NaOH (5ml) + water (300ml).

Solvent systems and polarity

The distance which a compound travels up a tlc plate depends on two factors, its polarity and that of the solvent. In the same solvent, the more polar the compound, the more tightly it is bound to the silica (or alumina) and the less it travels. There are some common trends, and with experience, it is often possible to predict whether a product will be less or more polar than the starting material. For example when a ketone, or ester is reduced, the resultant alcohol is almost always significantly more polar, and a clean transformation to a lower running spot will indicate a successful reaction. If the polarity of the solvent used for elution is increased the spots will move further up the plate and the distance between the centres of the spots usually increases, up to about half way up the plate. However, the spots also become more defuse, the further they travel, so an R$_f$ value of about 0.4 is normally the optimum for analytical purposes.

⚡The best tlc solvent system for a particular compound or mixture can only be determined by trial and error. However it is good practice to stick to a 'standard' solvent mixture, which can be used most of the time and you are familiar with. The most widely used solvent mixtures are based on a non-polar hydrocarbon, such as 40/60 petroleum ether or hexane, with a polar constituent added in a proportion which gives a suitable polarity. Probably the most popular 'universal' tlc system is petroleum ether - ethyl acetate, the polarity of which is easily adjusted by changing the proportions of the two solvents. If the compounds being analysed will not travel in ethyl acetate mixtures, a more polar solvent such as ethanol is used as the additive. On the other hand, if the compounds travel too far a less polar additive such as petroleum ether is used.

The degree of separation between compounds will also vary according to the solvent used, so if compounds do not separate or give poor separation in one system, different systems should be tried. Where there are a number a compounds in a mixture it may be best to use two or more different systems, for resolving the polar and non-polar components.

Common tlc solvents fall into one of three categories based on polarity, with smaller variations within each category.

Very polar solvent additives: methanol > ethanol > isopropanol

All much more polar than:

Moderately polar additives: acetonitrile > ethyl acetate > chloroform > dichloromethane > diethyl ether > toluene

All much more polar than:

Non-polar solvents: cyclohexane, petroleum-ether, hexane, pentane

Most solvent systems consist of one of the non-polar solvents together with a solvent from one of the other classes. However, for very polar compounds, one of the moderately polar solvents can be used as the less polar constituent. An example of this is chloroform - methanol mixtures, which are useful for highly hydroxylated compounds. The chlorinated hydrocarbons are also commonly used as single components.

Rf values

The Rf value of a compound depends upon the conditions under which the plate was run and is only accurate to about 20%, therefore it is best to compare compounds on the same plate, and run a mixed spot. However, it is useful to record the Rf value of a compound, *remembering to quote the solvent system.*

$$R_f = \frac{\text{Distance of centre of the spot from the baseline}}{\text{Distance of solvent front from baseline}}$$

Multiple elutions

It is sometimes useful to elute a particular tlc plate several times and so improve the separation of closely running spots. In practice this is done by eluting the tlc plate as normal, removing it from the tlc tank and allowing the solvent to evaporate from it, and then re-eluting the plate as before. Eluting a plate n-times is effectively the same as running a plate n-times its length.

Running acidic or basic compounds

Acidic and basic compounds often streak up the tlc plate. However, they will usually form distinct spots if, for acids a small amount of a carboxylic acid (e.g. acetic acid) is added to the solvent system, and for bases a small amount of amine (e.g. triethylamine) is added.

Running acid sensitive compounds

The silica on tlc plates is acidic in nature, and so compounds that are sensitive to acid may well decompose on tlc. There are several ways of getting around this problem, you can use alumina tlc plates (these suffer from the disadvantage that resolution is generally not as good, and the plates are basic in nature), or alternatively you can add a small amount of an amine (usually ammonia or triethylamine) to the solvent mixture to neutralize the acidic sites on the silica.

Checking for decomposition

Some organic compounds do decompose on silica to some extent, if you suspect that this is happening you can check by running a two-dimensional plate. This is done by cutting a square plate (ca. 5cm x 5cm) and spotting the compound in the bottom left-hand corner (ca. 0.5cm from the bottom) as shown in Fig. 8.16a. The plate is then eluted as normal to give the spots in a line up the left-hand side of the plate. The plate is then removed from the tlc tank and the solvent allowed to evaporate. It is then placed back in the tank with the line of spots along the bottom, and re-eluted (Fig. 8.16b).

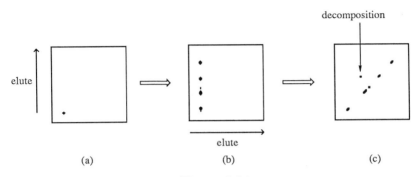

Figure 8.16

The result, if no decomposition is occurring will be the tlc running diagonally across the square plate, however if decomposition is occurring, the spot due to the unstable compound will show decomposition products off-diagonal (Fig. 8.16c).

It is very useful to carry out this test before any form of preparative chromatography, if you suspect that a compound may be labile on silica.

8.3.2 High performance liquid chromatography (hplc)

There is a broad range of hplc techniques, and many different types of equipment. It is beyond the scope of this book to describe in great detail the methods for operating the equipment. This section will therefore focus on some of the ways that hplc can be used to aid the synthetic organic chemist.

Description of hplc

The general arrangement of an hplc system is fairly simple, as shown in Fig. 8.17.

Solvent is pumped from a reservoir through a piston pump, which controls the flow rate. From the pump the solvent passes through a pulse damper, which removes some of the pulsing effect generated in the pump

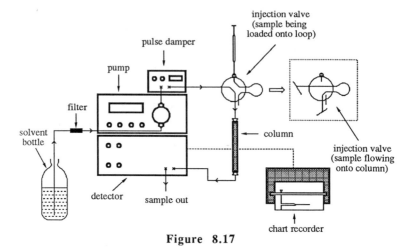

Figure 8.17

and also acts as a pressure regulator. In between the pulse damper and the column there is an injection valve which allows the sample to be introduced into the solvent stream. In the 'load' mode the solvent by-passes a sample loop, into which the sample is injected from a syringe. On switching to 'inject', the solvent stream is diverted through the load loop, introducing a very accurately measured volume of the sample solution onto the column. Components are separated on the hplc column in exactly the same way as they would be on a tlc plate, the less polar compounds running faster and coming through first. The effluent from the column passes into a detector (usually an ultraviolet or refractive index) which produces a signal on the chart recorder when a component is present.

The time at which the compound comes off the column is characteristic of that particular material, and is referred to as the retention time.

The area under any peak on the chart recorder is proportional to the quantity of that component and the method is therefore quantitative.

Uses of analytical hplc

Finding a tlc system and running a sample can be done very quickly and for this reason tlc is the normal method of choice for routine reaction monitoring. However, there are occasions when it is worth spending the time to set up an hplc system for reaction monitoring, especially if, as in many modern synthetic labs, you have a system close to hand. One reason to use hplc is that the compounds in which you are interested do not separate very well on tlc. The other common reason is that you require a quantitative technique. This may be the case if you are trying to optimize a reaction to maximize the quantity of one product over another, and for this type of extended study it is well worth the time it takes to set up the system. For most synthetic purposes it is the relative, rather than the absolute proportions of substances which are important, and if that is the case a simple comparison of integrated peak areas may be all that is required. If accurate quantification is needed, then a calibration is required and this can be done using an internal standard (see below).

Another common use of hplc is for identification of a compound by comparison with a known substance. Under a specific set of conditions (solvent, flow rate and quantity applied) any compound will have a specific retention time and this can therefore be used as a characteristic of the compound. However, just as a mixed spot should be always be run when comparing substances on tlc, so with hplc a single enhanced peak should be observed when the comparison substance and the unknown are injected as a mixture. Again caution should be used, since a single peak is not absolute proof that compounds are the same.

Preparative hplc is now becoming widely used in organic chemistry for separating compounds with very similar polarity (see Chapter 9 for more details). Before committing all your material to a preparative column it is always best to run a small quantity of the sample on an analytical column, in order to work out the best conditions. Indeed, columns are produced in various sizes which are directly comparable with one another.

If you are monitoring a reaction by hplc and you want to know the identity of one or more of the products, you can often separate a few milligrams from a few runs on the analytical column, which is enough to get a full range of spectral data. On simple hplc systems this can be done manually by collecting the effluent from the column when the peak of interest is coming off, and repeating several times. On more sophisticated systems a fraction collector is often incorporated and in some cases injections can be made automatically, so that the system can be set up to collect a particular peak or peaks over a large number of runs.

Several methods are now available for coupling an hplc system to a mass spectrometer, so that a mass spectrum is produced for each peak thus providing some structural information.

Quantitative analysis

For any type of detector each compound will have a different response, but for a particular compound, the area under its peak is directly proportional to the mass of material which produced the peak. If you are using a uv detector to analyse two compounds which have the same chromophore and extinction coefficients, then you can compare peak areas directly to determine the proportions of each compound.

Since the peak area is proportional to the mass of a compound, it is possible to take a known mass of a compound, make a standard solution and inject specific quantities, to work out the proportionality constant. However, a more accurate method of calibration is to use an internal standard. To do this follow the procedure below:

1. Choose as a standard a readily-available stable compound, with a retention time away from the peaks of interest.
2. Make up at least three mixtures containing known quantities of the standard and each of the compounds which are to be analysed.
3. Run the mixtures and measure the areas of each peak -
    The mass of material under any peak, y, is:

$$M_y = k_y \times Area_y$$

now, comparing the area under the standard peak with that under the unknown:

$$M_y/M_{(std)} = k_y/k_{(std)} \times Area_y/Area_{(std)}$$

Using this equation we can work out $k_y/k_{(std)}$ which is a constant k_y, known as the correction factor for compound y. Using data from each of the runs, the average correction factor for each compound is calculated.

4. Now if we want to calculate the quantity of a compound in a mixture, the mixture is spiked with a known quantity of the standard and the following equation is used:

$$M_y = k_y/M_{(std)} \times Area_y/Area_{(std)}$$

Peak shape

For good quantitative results from analytical hplc (or gc, see below) you should aim to produce chromatographs with symmetrical peaks. Tailing of the peaks is usually caused by overloading and can thus be avoided by reducing the quantity of sample applied. If this does not solve the problem and the tail of a component is long and drawn out, there may be an incompatibility between the compound and the stationary phase, a problem which is less easy to rectify.

Hplc can also be used for preparative separations and this is described in Chapter 9.

8.3.3 Gas-liquid chromatography (gc, glc, vpc)

Gas-liquid chromatography is becoming increasingly popular for reaction monitoring and for analysis of reaction products. It can be used for the analysis of any compounds which are volatile below about 300°C and thermally stable. It is not the intention of this section to give a detailed description of gc instrumentation, but simply to outline some of the uses of the technique for reaction monitoring and related work.

Description of gas chromatography

Gas chromatography is a very sensitive technique requiring only very small amounts of sample (10^{-6}g). A solution of about 1% is sufficient and a few microlitres of this is injected into a heated injector block. A stream of carrier gas, usually helium, passes through the injector and sweeps the vapours produced onto the column, which is contained in an oven. The temperature

Figure 8.18

of the oven can be accurately controlled and can either be kept constant or increased at a specified rate. Separation of the components in gc is not based on the principle of adsorption, as it is in liquid chromatography, but on partition. A gc column is rather like an extremely effective distillation column with the relative volatility of the components being the main factor which determines how quickly they travel through the column. The stationary phase of the column is a very high molecular weight, non-volatile oil, which has a very large surface area (see below for more detail about columns) and the gaseous components of the mixture are partitioned between the oil and the carrier gas at different rates. Thus the components are separated along the length of the column and emerge as discrete bands. The gas stream passing out of the column enters a flame ionization detector (FID) which produces an electric current when a compound is burned in the its flame. The electric current is amplified to produce a peak on the chart recorder. These detectors are very sensitive and the response produced is proportional to the quantity of material being burned, thus the peak area is proportional to the quantity of sample. As with hplc, the time taken for a particular substance to reach the detector is characteristic of that substance, and referred to as the retention time.

Types of gc column

A gc column must contain a liquid stationary phase with a large surface area, which must be supported, so that it stays in the column and the gas can pass through it. Packed columns are the traditional type, they are made from metal or glass coils, and have an internal diameter of about 2 to 4mm. The stationary liquid phase is coated on particles of solid with which the column is packed. There are a wide variety of stationary phases available ranging from Apiezon greases, which are very non-polar to polyethylene glycols which are very polar. With packed columns the choice of stationary phase is often critical for good separation and a good deal of experimentation is usually required before the best material is found.

The development of modern capillary columns has led to improved resolution and has also simplified the process of running gcs considerably. The columns are normally made from fused silica capillary with an inside diameter of between 0.2 and 0.5mm, and are polymer coated. They have no packing, but instead the liquid stationary phase is bonded to the inside wall of the capillary, and this allows gas to flow very easily. Because of this the columns can be made much longer than packed columns (between 12 and 100m) and they are typically ten times as efficient. Capillary columns give extremely high sensitivity and only a very small quantity of material is required. For this reason the injector normally incorporates a 'splitter', so that only a small portion of the sample injected actually enters the column.

The development of capillary columns has been largely responsible for the increased use of gc for monitoring organic reactions and for product analysis. The increased sensitivity of these columns is one important reason for this, but the fact that they are very simple to set up and operate is perhaps more significant. The type of stationary phase is not so critical as with packed columns and the gas flow rate is essentially determined by the column, so the instrument can be operated successfully with minimal prior expertise. For most purposes relating to preparative organic chemistry it is sufficient to rely on just two types of column, one non-polar (such as a BP1) and one polar column (such as a BP20).

Uses of gc for reaction monitoring and product analysis

Capillary gc instruments are so simple to use that, provided there is one close by, monitoring a reaction by gc is almost as quick as running a tlc. It is common to turn to gc monitoring when tlc does not provide resolution between starting material and product or between one product and another. Gc will usually separate components which co-run on tlc. We also find that some compounds, such as amines, which do not run very well on tlc, can be analysed very easily by capillary gc.

Gc also provides quantitative analysis and is widely used for determination of product ratios from diastereoselective reactions, down to about 200:1. This makes it an ideal technique for optimization studies, where a large number of small-scale reactions are carried out under different conditions and product ratios are measured simply by syringing out a few microlitres from each and then injecting into the gc instrument earlier.

For absolute quantitative studies the gc instrument can be calibrated in exactly the same way as described for the hplc instrument. Some people use this technique to measure theoretical yields for reactions, although it is always preferable that isolated yields are quoted.

The identity of a compound can often be determined by gc, if an unknown has the same retention time, and co-runs with a known compound when the two are injected as a mixture, but just as with tlc and hplc co-running, caution should be exercised. A very powerful structure analysis technique is gc mass specrometry (gc-ms) and when capillary gc is used this is a very simple and quick form of analysis. The mass spectrometer simply acts as the detector, but as well as providing a chromatograph, a mass spectrum of each individual component is obtained. Capillary gc-ms is a very sensitive technique and mass spectroscopic data can be obtained even on very minor components of a mixture.

One example of how gc and gc-ms can be useful is shown in Fig. 8.19. The first time this reaction was carried out, tlc analysis indicated that the starting material had been completely transformed to a single product, which ran as one spot in a number of solvent systems, but the product did not appear to be pure by ^{1}H nmr spectroscopy. When a gc-ms was run on the reaction product, two compounds (which ran together on tlc) were separated and easily distinguished as compounds A and C. Also, 3% of isomeric compound B was identified and although this runs separately from A and C on tlc it had not been detected previously due to lack of sensitivity.

A   B   C

Figure 8.19

Having discovered the identity of the reaction products by gc-ms, product ratios for a series of reaction were obtained using simple gc and we were thus able to find optimum conditions for generation of compound A.

In this section we have not endeavoured to give a comprehensive review of methods which can be used for reaction monitoring, but we have described the most universal and commonly used modern techniques. Various other monitoring methods can be devised for specific reactions. For instance ultraviolet (uv) spectroscopy can be used if one strong chromophore is being converted to another, but the disadvantage of spectroscopic methods is that they do not indicate how many products are being produced. Nmr spectroscopy can also be employed and this is mentioned further in Chapter 10.

8.4 Reactions at other than room temperature

In many cases it is necessary to carry out reactions at non-ambient temperatures. Usually reactions that are exothermic or involve the intermediacy of thermally-unstable species have to be carried out at low temperatures, typically in the range 0°C to -100°C. Similarly, reactions that are endothermic or have high energies of activation have to be carried out at higher temperatures, typically in the range 30°C to 180°C although in some cases temperatures exceeding 300°C may be necessary. This section deals with the techniques involved in such situations.

8.4.1 Low temperature reactions

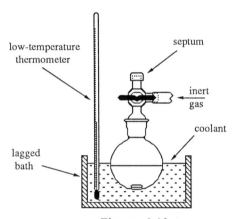

Figure 8.20

Reactions are usually carried out below room temperature by placing the reaction vessel in a cooling bath. In general this is done by placing a cooling mixture into a lagged bath, and then immersing the reaction vessel in the cooling mixture to a depth that ensures the reaction contents are below the level of coolant (Fig. 8.20). The temperature of the coolant can be monitored by means of a low temperature thermometer immersed in the bath. It should be noted when carrying out reactions using cooling baths, that the reaction itself may not be at the same temperature as the bath due to exothermic processes taking place, so where possible the internal reaction temperature should also be monitored. A particularly convenient way of doing this is to use a digital low-temperature thermometer. These are

Figure 8.21

commercially available, and most come with a hypodermic probe which can be inserted into the reaction flask through a septum (Fig. 8.21). The temperature can then be noted and the probe withdrawn. This is often a much easier procedure than the more usual method of setting up the reaction apparatus to include an internal thermometer, and is particularly useful for small-scale set-ups where an internal thermometer cannot be used.

In general all low temperature reactions should be done under inert atmosphere (nitrogen or argon) to avoid atmospheric moisture from being condensed into the reaction mixture.

The three main types of cooling mixtures are described below:

i)   Ice-salt baths. Various salts or solvents can be mixed with crushed ice to produce sub-zero temperatures. In practice, temperatures ranging from 0°C to -40°C can be obtained (see Table 8.1); however at the lower temperatures the cooling mixture consists of granular ice-salt particles with little or no liquid, and so this can result in poor thermal contact with any vessel immersed in it. For the lower temperatures, where careful temperature control is important, it is preferable to use a liquid or slush coolant which has good thermal contact with any vessel immersed in it.

Table 8.1: Ice-based cold baths[1]

Additive	Ratio (ice/additive)	Temperature °C
Water	1:1	0
NaCl	3:1	-8
Acetone	1:1	-10
$CaCl_2.6H_2O$	4:5	-40

ii) Dry ice-solvent baths. Solid carbon dioxide (dry ice) is commercially available as pellets or blocks, and forms very good cooling mixtures when combined with a variety of organic solvents (see Table 8.2). In practice the baths are prepared by adding the dry ice pellets carefully to a bath containing the requisite solvent until the temperature required is reached. The temperatures quoted in Table 8.2 refer to baths in which an excess of dry ice is contained in the solvent. In this case cooling mixtures ranging from -15°C to -78°C can be achieved.

Table 8.2: Dry-ice cold baths[2]

Solvent	Temperature °C	Solvent	Temperature °C
Ethylene glycol	-15	Chloroform	-61
Carbon tetrachloride	-25	Ethanol	-72
Heptan-3-one	-38	Acetone	-78
Acetonitrile	-42		

iii) Liquid nitrogen slush baths. Slush baths are made by adding liquid nitrogen carefully to a solvent contained in the bath, with continuous stirring (glass rod, not a thermometer). The coolant should become the consistency of ice-cream, and stirring should prevent any solidification. Again a variety of different liquids can be used to give temperatures ranging from 13°C to -196°C (see Table 8.3). Such cooling systems can often be left for several hours if the cooling bath is well lagged, however for longer periods (overnight) some form of mechanical cooling is usually necessary. In such instances, the reaction vessel can

1. A.J. Gordon and R.A. Ford, "The Chemist's Companion", J. Wiley and Sons, New York, 1972.
2. A.M. Phillips and D.N. Hume, *J. Chem. Ed.*, 1968, **54**, 664.

be placed in a refrigerator, or cooled by the use of a portable commercial refrigeration unit.

Table 8.3: Liquid nitrogen slush baths[3]

Solvent	Temperature °C	Solvent	Temperature °C
p-Xylene	13	Chloroform	-63
p-Dioxane	12	Isopropyl acetate	-73
Cyclohexane	6	Butyl acetate	-77
Formamide	2	Ethyl acetate	-84
Aniline	-6	2-Butanone	-86
Diethylene glycol	-10	Isopropanol	-89
Cycloheptane	-12	n-Propyl acetate	-92
Benzyl alcohol	-15	Hexane	-94
o-Dichlorobenzene	-18	Toluene	-95
Carbon tetrachloride	-23	Methanol	-98
o-Xylene	-29	Cyclohexene	-104
m-Toluidine	-32	Isooctane	-107
Thiophene	-38	Carbon disulphide	-110
Acetonitrile	-41	Ethanol	-116
Chlorobenzene	-45	Methyl cyclohexane	-126
m-Xylene	-47	n-Pentane	-131
Benzyl acetate	-52	Isopentane	-160
n-Octane	-56	Liquid nitrogen	-196

8.4.2 Reactions above room temperature

1. Reactions in a sealed tube

Reactions above room temperature usually require modifications to the standard equipment set-up. In some instances the reaction can be performed in a sealed tube, usually made of thick-walled glass. The reaction mixture is placed in the tube which is then sealed, placed in an oven and heated to the appropriate temperature (Fig. 8.22). After the reaction is complete, the tube is cooled, opened and the contents removed. Such a technique is employed when temperatures in excess of the solvent boiling point are required, or for reactions involving extremely volatile compounds. This technique naturally

3. R.E. Rondeau, *J. Chem. Eng. Data*, 1966, **11**, 124.

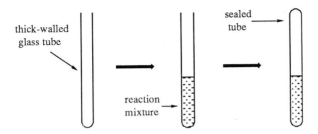

Figure 8.22

requires a high degree of skill, since heating leads to a pressure build-up inside the tube which can result in explosion if there are any flaws in the seal.

Figure 8.23

An alternative to the all-glass sealed tube is to use a reaction tube, which consists of a thick-walled glass tube with a teflon screw seal at the top (Fig. 8.23). This serves as a re-usable sealed tube apparatus, and commercial versions of this apparatus are available. It also features a useful side-arm that allows evacuation or purging with an inert gas prior to sealing the tube.

2. Reactions involving the use of a condenser

For most reactions above room temperature, an open system which does not
lead to a build-up of pressure is employed. This usually consists of a

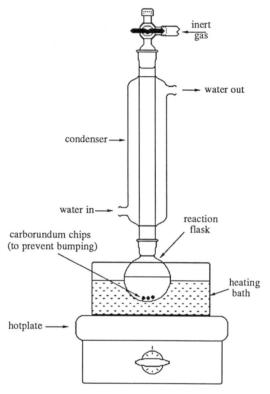

Figure 8.24

reaction vessel protected with a condenser (Fig. 8.24). The condenser is
used to prevent the evaporation of volatile materials (usually the solvent)
from the reaction mixture.

There are many different designs of condenser available, and the type
used depends upon the nature of the reaction involved. The most common
designs of condenser are the Liebig condenser (Fig. 8.25a), the coiled
condenser (Fig. 8.25b), the double-jacketed coiled condenser (Fig. 8.25c),
and the cold-finger condenser (Fig. 8.25d). Other condensers available tend
to be simple modifications of these three types.

The Liebig condenser, the coiled condenser, and the double-jacketed
coiled condenser are similar in design and function. They are water-cooled

via connection to a cold-water tap, in the case of the Liebig condenser the water flows in at the bottom and flows out at the top giving a jacket of cold water around the condenser stem and leading to a cold surface on the inside. Any volatile materials in the reaction condense on the cold outer surface and

(a)   (b)   (c)   (d)

Figure 8.25

run back into the reaction mixture. The coiled condenser functions in a similar way only now the cold surface is on the inside of the condenser. This can offer an advantage in particularly humid locations because there is less tendency for atmospheric moisture to condense on the outside of the condenser and run down over the reaction vessel. The double-jacketed coiled condenser is also water-cooled, again water flows in at the bottom and out at the top. This condenser design tends to be more efficient than the other two because it provides a greater area of cold surface. Consequently it is preferred when low boiling materials (≤ 40°C) are involved.

The cold-finger condenser is rather different from the above three. It is cooled by either solid carbon dioxide / acetone (-78°C) or liquid nitrogen (-196°C). The coolant is placed in the top of the condenser and more coolant is added as required. This results in an extremely cold surface on the inside of the condenser. Condensers of this type are usually employed for reactions that involve solvents or components that boil at or below room temperature (e.g. liquid ammonia, b.p. -33°C), although they can be used for higher boiling materials as well.

3. Heating devices

As with low-temperature reactions, a common method of increasing the temperature of a reaction is to place the reaction flask in a bath (Fig. 8.23). In this case the contents of the bath are then heated, usually using a hotplate.

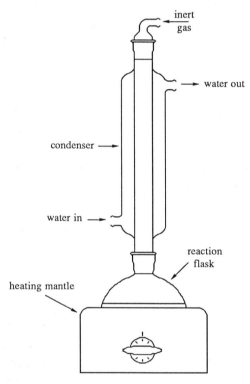

Figure 8.26

There are four commonly employed heating baths; water, silicone oil, Woods metal, flaked graphite, and sand. Water baths consist of a pyrex glass container filled with water, and are used for reactions requiring temperatures up to 100°C. Silicone oil baths are similar in design but can be used for temperatures up to about 180°C, although the maximum temperature in this case depends upon the precise type of oil employed. Woods metal is a commercially available alloy (50% Bi, 25% Pb, 12.5% Sn, 12.5% Cd) that melts at 70°C. It has excellent thermal properties and so is a safe material for use at quite high temperatures (up to 300°C). It is normally used in a steel container, and again heated via a hot-plate device.

Similarly, flaked graphite and sand can be used in heating baths up to 300°C, although they cool slowly compared with the Woods metal.

Reactions can also be heated by an electric heating mantle (Fig. 8.26), although in general this is less satisfactory since it is more difficult to control the temperature of the mantle surface and excessive heating of the reaction flask can result. Because of this, where possible heating mantles should be avoided for reactions below 100°C although they can be used if necessary.

8.5 Driving equilibria

A number of important organic reactions involve equilibria and do not give good yields unless the equilibrium can be shifted to the product side. An equilibrium can be driven to the right by using an excess of one of the reactants, by continuously removing one of the products, or by changing the temperature or the pressure at which the reaction is carried out. In most cases use of excess reagent or removal of a product can be achieved usingnormal apparatus and techniques. This section is concerned with two methods which involve special apparatus; Dean and Stark traps, and high pressure reactors.

8.5.1 Dean and Stark traps

Perhaps the most commonly encountered equilibrium reactions are those involving water as a reactant or product. Driving such equilibria by using excess water (e.g. hydrolysis reactions) is easy, but driving equilibria by removing water (e.g. in ester or acetal formation) can be more difficult. An excellent device for the continuous removal of water from a reaction mixture is the Dean and Stark trap (Fig. 8.27). The apparatus is assembled as shown and the reaction is conducted in a solvent which forms an azeotrope with water (almost invariably a hydrocarbon such as toluene). When the mixture is heated the solvent/water azeotrope distils over and, on condensing, is collected in the trap. The water then separates and the light organic solvent flows back into the reaction flask. It is usually easy to monitor the progress of the reaction either by recording the volume of water produced or by waiting until the characteristically milky heterogeneous azeotrope is no longer produced.

condenser

Dean-Stark
trap

reaction flask

heating bath

Figure 8.27   A Dean and Stark trap

A Dean and Stark trap can also be used to remove volatile alcohols, such as methanol and ethanol, which *are* miscible with many organic solvents. They can nevertheless be removed by placing 5Å molecular sieves (Section 4.3) in the trap, in order to absorb the alcohol. An alternative is use a Soxhlet extractor containing molecular sieves.

On a small scale, simply placing some activated sieves in the reaction flask is a convenient means of removing water. This method is effective in driving equilibria and is also used to promote reactions which are adversely affected by water.

8.5.2 High pressure reactions

A more esoteric technique is to carry out the reaction at very high pressures (>10kbar), thus shifting the equilibrium to the side of the components which have the smaller volume. Some transformation of the products must be carried out as soon as they are removed from the reactor, in order to prevent re-equilibration. A recent review[1] gives an account of some applications of high pressure techniques.

1. N.S. Isaacs and A.V. George, *Chem. Br.*, 1987, **23**, 47.

8.6   Agitation

For homogeneous reaction systems at constant temperature, agitation is not normally necessary.   However, most reactions involve heterogeneous reaction mixtures and so require some form of agitation to ensure efficient mixing of the reactants. The most commonly used methods of agitation are outlined in this section.

8.6.1 Magnetic stirring

Magnetic stirrer machines are commonly available and come in two general types: either a simple stirring machine, or one that also incorporates a hotplate for heating reaction systems (Fig. 8.28). They consist of a box containing a motor that drives an electromagnet which spins horizontally. Most magnetic stirrers have a flat top to allow cooling or heating baths (see Section 4.6) to be placed on top.   Agitation of the reaction mixture is achieved by placing a magnetic stirrer bar (or follower) in the reaction mixture.   The reaction vessel is then clamped over the top of the stirrer machine in such a position as to allow the mixture to be stirred by magnetic interaction of the follower with the electromagnet in the stirrer machine. Usually the rate of stirring can be adjusted using a control on the stirrer machine.

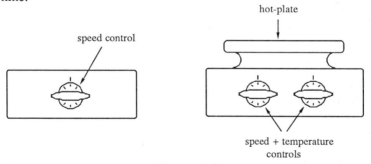

Figure 8.28

The follower consists of a magnet coated with an inert polymer, usually Teflon or PVC, and come in a variety of shapes and sizes (Fig. 8.29) It is important that the polymer coating does not react with any components in the reaction mixture, and because of this Teflon is usually the preferred coating. The size of the follower is also important, it should be large enough to stir the reaction mixture effectively but not so large that it will not sit flat in the bottom of the reaction flask.

(a)   (b)   (c)

Figure 8.29 Magnetic followers: (a) bar; (b) octagonal; (c) egg-shaped

Because the follower is driven by a magnetic field and has no mechanical connection with the stirrer machine, this method of agitation does not require special modification of a reaction apparatus.

Magnetic stirrer machines are probably the most commonly employed method of agitation for organic reactions, but can become ineffective if particularly viscous systems are encountered. They may also be ineffective if the reaction vessel has to be placed inside another piece of apparatus such as a heating mantle or large cooling bath. In such cases the extra apparatus can effectively shield the reaction flask from the magnetic field created by the stirrer machine. Magnetic stirring can also be a problem for large scale reactions (reaction volumes over one litre), and in such cases mechanical stirring is a valuable alternative.

8.6.2 Mechanical stirrers

Mechanical stirring machines consist of an electric motor clamped above the reaction vessel, that rotates a vertical rod (usually glass, although it can be steel or Teflon). A vane or paddle is attached to the bottom of this rod, and it is this that is responsible for agitation of the reaction mixture (Fig. 8.30) The rod and vane are usually detachable enabling different length rods and different sized vanes to be used as appropriate. As with magnetic stirrer machines, the rate of stirring can usually be adjusted by means of a control on the motor. There are many different designs for the vane, the most common being a crescent shaped piece of Teflon about 5mm thick. This has a slot in it that allows easy attachment to the glass rod (Fig. 8.31). In this design the vane can be rotated about a horizontal axis and so can easily be put through the narrow neck of a round-bottomed flask, then rotated into a horizontal position ready for use.

Figure 8.30

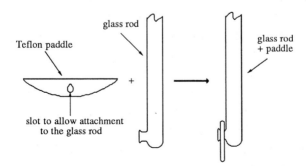

Figure 8.31

Because the mechanical stirrer requires a physical attachment to the reaction flask, precautions have to be taken if the reaction is to be carried out under anhydrous conditions, or under an inert gas atmosphere. The usual way of doing this is to use a stirrer guide that allows the rod to enter the reaction flask, but prevents atmospheric gases from doing so. These are constructed from Teflon (Fig.8.32a), and provide a tight fit between a ground glass joint and the glass rod. The tight seal around the rod is achieved by means of an O-ring seal inside the stirrer guide, and a set-up of this type should be good enough to withstand a vacuum of 0.5-0.1mmHg inside the reaction flask without leaking. Because the guide is constructed entirely from Teflon it does not require lubrication.

Figure 8.32

Such guides are necessarily expensive, and for many uses that do not require rigorously controlled reaction conditions a glass guide can be employed (Fig. 8.32b). This consists of a precision-ground glass tube attached to a normal ground glass joint. In this case it is essential to use a ground glass rod that forms a good fit with the tube. Oil lubrication is required to allow the rod to rotate, and so this set-up is not suitable for reactions above room temperature that involve volatile solvents which can leach the lubricant into the reaction mixture.

Because mechanical stirrers use an electric motor mounted above the reaction flask, there is a serious danger of sparks from the motor igniting volatile flammable solvents. In such instances the use of mechanical stirrers powered by compressed air is recommended.

8.6.3 Mechanical shakers

reaction flask

counter balance
flask

Figure 8.33

Mechanical shakers come in many designs, and are simply motors that will shake an attached reaction flask. The flask is usually clamped to the shaker (Fig. 8.33), often with a counter-weight to balance the machine. This is a useful device for reactions that involve vigorous mixing of two immiscible liquids for prolonged periods of time, and can also be employed when efficient mixing of a gas and liquid are required (e.g. hydrogenation); however, for most applications other methods of agitation are preferable.

8.6.4 Sonication

septum

inert
gas

reaction flask

water

ultrasonic
bath

Figure 8.34

Ultrasonic waves can also be employed as a means of agitation. This most common arrangement is to use a simple ultrasonic bath, in which the reaction vessel is placed (Fig. 8.34), although ultrasonic probes can also be used and are often placed inside the reaction vessel (Fig. 8.35). The latter arrangement is particularly desirable if precise control of the ultrasound frequency is required, or if external control of the reaction temperature is necessary. In both cases ultrasonic waves are generated inside the reaction vessel, causing agitation of its contents. This technique is particularly useful for reactions involving insoluble solids. The ultrasonic waves break up the solids into very small particles facilitating solvolysis and reaction.

Figure 8.35

CHAPTER 9

Working Up The Reaction

9.1   Introduction

It is important to give some thought to the work up of the reaction before you attempt it. There are several aspects which need to be considered which will be dealt with here. First of all do make sure that the reaction has indeed finished (by careful analysis using your chosen monitoring system). When using tlc analysis it is sometimes difficult to judge by spotting the reaction mixture directly on to the tlc plate. In these cases it is often possible to get a more accurate assessment by withdrawing a small aliquot of reaction mixture by syringe and adding it to a small vial containing a few drops each of ether and aqueous ammonium chloride. Agitation followed by tlc of the organic phase will often give clean, reliable tlc information. This technique can also be used to screen alternative work up conditions, for example adding to water or aqueous base rather than ammonium chloride solution, or using other organic solvents in place of ether.

Having satisfied yourself that the reaction has run to completion, or that it is time to end the experiment, the appropriate 'quench' is added to the reaction mixture. Choice of this reagent can be very important in determining the yield of desired product, and it is obviously vital to use a reagent or procedure which is safe. Given that the product is expected to be reasonably stable, which usually is the case, then the choice of procedure for quenching the reaction is determined by the reagent(s) used in the reaction. Clearly we cannot cover all possibilities in this chapter, but general procedures which should cover most of the situations that are likely to be encountered are provided below. The classification is made on the basis of the nature of the reaction mixture which is to be worked up.

9.2   Quenching the reaction

9.2.1 General comments

If the reaction has been carried out under an inert atmosphere then it is advisable to add the quench before exposing the reaction mixture to the air. It is best added as you would add a reagent, dropwise by syringe. If the reaction was run at low temperature, then add the quench at this temperature and allow to warm to room temperature slowly before opening to the air and proceeding with the isolation of the product. If the reaction was run at elevated temperature, allow to cool before adding the quench (still under the inert atmosphere if used). If an exotherm is possible, ensure that the reaction is cooled in a cooling bath (e.g. ice/water) if it is not already in a low temperature bath, and that the quench is added very carefully (if the scale of the reaction is such that an internal thermometer can be used, then do so and keep a close eye on the internal temperature while quenching the reaction).

These general comments apply to the following specific types of reactions. Obviously if a known, fully described literature procedure is being used, then follow the work up and isolation process exactly. Only modify such a procedure if you encounter problems.

9.2.2 Strongly basic non-aqueous reactions

This is a common type of reaction, typical examples would include alkylation using strong bases (e.g. BuLi, (i-Pr)$_2$NLi), many organometallic reagents (e.g. MeLi, Grignard reagents), hydride reducing agents (e.g. LiAlH$_4$, Na(EtOCH$_2$CH$_2$O)$_2$AlH$_2$), and cuprate reactions. The most commonly used quench for this type of reaction is an excess of aqueous ammonium chloride, added slowly, to protonate anions present and to destroy excess or unreacted reagent. This can be added at low temperatures, but if you are concerned about the aqueous solution freezing out (there is usually no need to worry about this in our experience) then use acetic acid as the quench. Make sure that enough is added to destroy all the reagent and to protonate any anions which might be present, but do not add too much as it can sometimes make isolation and purification of the product more difficult.

In the case of aluminium based reagents such as LiAlH$_4$ and (i-Bu)$_2$AlH, alternative procedures are often used to attempt to avoid very fine precipitates which are difficult to filter and which can lead to emulsions. One simple method which often gives good results is to add a saturated aqueous solution of sodium sulphate dropwise with stirring (and cooling!), until a very heavy precipitate is formed (do not add excess solution just to 'make sure'). The supernatant can then be decanted and the solid extracted a few times with the reaction solvent, combining all the organics. (If you try this, do not dispose of the solid until you are certain that you have obtained a good recovery of material. It might be necessary to extract further to obtain all of the product).

9.2.3 Neutral non-aqueous reactions

'Neutral' is taken to cover all reactions which involve neither strong base or acid. Such a 'neutral' reaction might be in fact slightly acidic (e.g. acid-catalysed ketalisation) or slightly basic (e.g. tosylation of an alcohol using pyridine or triethylamine as the base). Clearly a great many reactions fall into this category and in general the quench can be ammonium chloride solution or water for mildly basic reactions, and dilute sodium hydrogen carbonate for mildly acidic reactions.

If a fairly reactive reagent has been used then add the quench carefully with cooling. For example if p-toluene sulphonyl chloride has been used to prepare a tosylate, it is useful to add a relatively small volume of water and stir for an hour or so to destroy any remaining sulphonyl chloride (be certain to add at least enough to destroy all of the sulphonyl chloride which was used). This will convert the chloride to the sulphonic acid (present as a salt with the amine used in the reaction) which is easy to remove in the subsequent extraction and purification.

As ever, it is important to be certain that your product is unlikely to be sensitive to (or destroyed by) the quench. For example any reaction which has been driven to completion by removal of water needs some thought. A common example of this is acid-catalysed ketalisation. The product ketal is likely to be sensitive to aqueous acid, so be sure to quench with plenty of aqueous sodium hydrogen carbonate solution before proceeding with the isolation.

9.2.4 Strongly acidic non-aqueous reactions

This type of reaction will usually involve the use of a strong Lewis acid such as $TiCl_4$ or $BF_3.OEt_2$. It is important to be aware that the addition of water to these reagents will be exothermic and usually liberates strong protic acid. If the product is likely to be unaffected by the liberated acid, then water can be used as a quench. It is often the case that the product will be unstable towards this acid, or at least to contain functionality which will be destroyed by acid, and in this case aqueous sodium bicarbonate or carbonate can be used. If a non-aqueous quench is desired then a solution of gaseous ammonia in the reaction solvent can be used. Quench these reactions carefully, with cooling, and be aware that the metals used (Ti and Al particularly) can give rise to insoluble precipitates and be prepared to deal with the problems which these might cause (see below).

9.2.5 Acidic or basic aqueous reactions

To quench these reactions it is usually enough to neutralize with dilute acid or base, but do consider the product which you wish to isolate. For example if you are hydrolyzing an ester then no quench will be required, the desired product will be isolated by the appropriate extraction procedure.

9.2.6 Liquid ammonia reactions

A number of synthetically useful reactions use this as solvent, and usually involve either the use of, or generation of strongly basic species. The usual quench for this type of reaction is to add (*carefully*) an excess solid ammonium chloride, and allowing the ammonia to evaporate (*fume cupboard*).

Conclusion

In conclusion, the correct quench for a reaction is usually simple to determine, given that adequate consideration is given to the reagents used and the product expected. If you are at all unsure, then remove a small quantity of the reaction mixture and add it to a vial containing a few drops of both the quench and the reaction solvent and observe. Tlc analysis (or whatever analytical technique was used to monitor the reaction) will be useful in ensuring that all is well (or otherwise). It is better to 'waste' a little product in this way than to lose it all by incorrect choice of quench.

With the reaction successfully quenched, then the isolation of product can be carried out, as outlined below.

9.3 Isolation of the crude product

9.3.1 General comments

The usual isolation procedure involves partitioning the reaction mixture between an organic solvent and water (or aqueous solutions). Before carrying this out it is often useful to remove any solid which is present. It can be particularly important to remove very fine particles, even if they are present in a small amount, as these can lead to emulsions forming in subsequent extractions. This is best achieved by dilution of the (quenched) reaction mixture with the reaction solvent followed by vacuum filtration through a Celite pad, made by packing Celite onto a sintered glass funnel (with the vacuum on). Do wash the pad thoroughly with water, followed by the solvent which you are using since Celite can contain soluble impurities. Simply filter the reaction mixture through this pad, and rinse through two or three times to ensure complete transfer of your product.

If your solvent has reasonable solubility in water then it is advisable to remove most or all of it at this stage on a rotary evaporator. This is not always necessary but omitting it can lead to losses of product to the aqueous phase during extraction. The most commonly encountered examples of this type of solvent are alcohols and tetrahydrofuran, and the problem gets worse as the polarity of the product increases.

The reaction mixture can now be partitioned between water (or an aqueous solution) and an organic solvent. Throughout the extraction procedure do not discard any extract until you have made sure that you have a good mass recovery (on weighing the crude product). If a low recovery is obtained the rest must be somewhere and it is likely that the product will be in one of the extracts. For most reactions dichloromethane can be used or diethyl ether if a solvent less dense than water is required. Dichloromethane is much safer than ether so use it whenever possible. If a low recovery is obtained with dichloromethane or ether, then simply extract the aqueous layers (which you have kept!) with either chloroform or ethyl acetate. These are more powerful solvents and will often extract polar compounds from aqueous solutions. If this fails, try saturating the aqueous extracts with sodium chloride and extracting again with chloroform or ethyl acetate. Whenever you extract with an organic solvent use several portions rather than one large one as this is much more efficient.

Occasionally you will encounter the problem of emulsions during extraction. There is no universal solution to this, but a common cause is the presence of very fine particles, which can be removed by filtration through Celite as described above. If this fails, try adding sodium chloride to the aqueous, and try adding another organic solvent.

9.3.2 Very polar aprotic solvents

The most commonly encountered of these are dimethyl sulphoxide (DMSO) and N,N-dimethylformamide (DMF). With these solvents it is often possible to remove most if not all by adding the quenched reaction mixture to a relatively large volume of water, and extracting this several times with ether. The combined organics are then washed with more water. Any remaining DMF or DMSO will need to be removed in further purification of the crude product.

With the extractions completed the organic extract needs to be dried. A lot of the dissolved water can be removed by extracting with saturated brine and it is advisable to do this. The organic extract is then dried fully by addition of either anhydrous magnesium or sodium sulphate and standing for an hour or so (or less if you are in a hurry!), followed by vacuum filtration through a sintered glass funnel.

The solvent is now usually removed using a rotary evaporator, with the final traces being removed using a high vacuum line. Beware when using the high vacuum line, if your product is volatile it will 'disappear' into the traps!

At this stage it is very useful *(after weighing!)* to examine the crude product by ir, nmr, and tlc before proceeding with purification as this will give you an idea as to the state of purity amongst other things. The rest of this chapter is given over to methods for purification of the crude product.

9.4   Purification

When a product has been isolated from a reaction the next step is to purify it. The degree of purity required will depend on the use for which the sample is intended, a synthetic intermediate might only require rough purification, whereas a product for elemental analysis would require rigorous purification. This section describes the most important purification techniques, crystallization, distillation, sublimation, and chromatography. It is assumed that the reader is familiar with the basic principles of these methods, so the emphasis is on more demanding applications such as the purification of air-sensitive materials, and purifications on a micro-scale.

9.4.1 Crystallization

Simple recrystallization of an impure solid is a routine operation, which nevertheless requires care and good judgement if good results are to be obtained. The basic procedure can be broken down into six steps, which are listed below, together with some tips on how to overcome common problems.

1.   Select a suitable solvent

Find a suitable solvent by carrying out small scale tests. Remember that 'like dissolves like'. The most commonly used solvents in order of increasing polarity are petroleum ether, toluene, chloroform, acetone, ethyl acetate, ethanol, and water. Chloroform and dichloromethane are rarely useful on their own because they are good solvents for the great majority of organic compounds. It is preferable to use a solvent with a boiling point in excess of 60°C, but the b.p. should be at least 10°C lower than the m.p. of the compound to be crystallized, in order to prevent the solute from 'oiling out' of solution. In many cases a mixed solvent must be used, and combinations of toluene, chloroform, or ethyl acetate, with the petroleum ether fraction of similar boiling point are particularly useful. Consult Appendix 1 for boiling points, polarity (dielectric constant), and toxicity of common solvents.

2.   Dissolve the compound in the minimum volume of hot solvent

Remember that most organic solvents are extremely flammable and that many produce very toxic vapour.

Place the crude compound (always keep a few 'seed' crystals) in a conical flask fitted with a reflux condenser, add boiling chips and a small portion of solvent, and heat in a water bath. Continue to add portions of solvent at intervals until all of the crude has dissolved in the hot/refluxing solvent. If you are using a mixed solvent, dissolve the crude in a small volume of the good solvent, heat to reflux, add the poor solvent in portions until the compound just begins to precipitate (cloudiness), add a few drops of the good solvent to redissolve the compound, and allow to cool.

When adding the solvent it is very easy to be misled into adding far too much if the crude is contaminated with an insoluble material such as silica or magnesium sulphate.

3. Filter the hot solution to remove insoluble impurities

This step is often problematic and should NOT be carried out unless an unacceptable (use your judgement) amount of insoluble material is suspended in the solution. The difficulty here is that the compound tends to crystallize during the filtration so an excess of solvent (ca. 5%) should be added, and the apparatus used for the filtration should be preheated to about the boiling point of the solvent. Use a clean sintered funnel of porosity 2 or 3, or a Hirsch or Buchner funnel, and use the minimum suction needed to draw the solution rapidly through the funnel.

If the solution is very dark and/or contains small amounts of tarry impurities, allow it to cool for a few moments, add ca. 2% by weight of decolorising charcoal, reflux for a few minutes, and filter off the charcoal. Charcoal is very finely divided so it is essential to put a 1 cm layer of a filter aid such as Celite on the funnel before filtering the suspension. Observe the usual precautions for preventing crystallization in the funnel. Very dark or tarry products should be chromatographed through a short (2-3cm) plug of silica before attempted recrystallization.

4. Allow the solution to cool and the crystals to form

This is usually straightforward except when the material is very impure or has a low m.p. ($< 40°C$) in which case it sometimes precipitates as an oil. If an oil forms it is best to reheat the solution and then to allow it to cool slowly. Try scratching the flask with a glass rod or adding a few 'seed' crystals to induce crystallization, and if this fails try adding some more solvent so that precipitation occurs at a lower temperature.

If nothing at all precipitates from the solution, try scratching with a glass rod, seeding, or cooling the solution in ice-water. If all these fail, stopper the flask and set it aside for a few days, patience is sometimes the best policy.

5. *Filter off and dry the crystals*

When crystallization appears to be complete filter off the crystals using an appropriately sized sintered glass funnel. It is very important to wash the crystals carefully. As soon as all of the mother liquor has drained through the funnel, remove the suction and pour some *cold* solvent over the crystals, stirring them if necessary, in order to ensure that they are thoroughly washed. Drain off the washing under suction and repeat once or twice more.

After careful washing allow the crystals to dry briefly in the air and then remove the last traces of solvent under vacuum, in a vacuum oven, in a drying pistol, or on a vacuum line. Take care to protect your crystals against accidental spillage or contamination. If they are placed in a dish, a beaker, or a sample vial, cover with aluminium foil, secure with wire or an elastic band, and punch a few small holes in the foil. If the crystals are in a flask connected directly to a vacuum line, use a tubing adapter with a tap and put a plug of glass wool in the upper neck of the adapter so that the crystals are not blown about or contaminated with rubbish from the tubing, when the air/inert gas is allowed in.

If a relatively high boiling solvent such as toluene was used for the recrystallization it is essential to heat the sample under vacuum for several hours to ensure that all of the solvent is removed.

Small scale crystallization

When small samples (less than 200mg) are to be recrystallized it is particularly important to remove traces of insoluble material and to avoid contamination by dust, filter paper, etc. Thus it is essential to use carefully cleaned glassware and purified solvents, and to filter the hot solution. The apparatus shown in Fig. 9.1 is convenient for small scale (5-200mg) recrystallizations. Place the sample in the bulb and wash it with a few drops of solvent. Heat the bulb in an oil bath or a water bath so that the solvent refluxes up to the level of the sintered disc. Add more solvent, in small portions, until the compound has dissolved. Remove the apparatus from the bath, wipe the bulb to remove oil or water, and quickly filter the hot solution into a clean receiver by pressurising the vessel using hand bellows or an inert gas line. Filtering under pressure in this way avoids the problem of unwanted crystallization, and reduces transfer losses.

Figure 9.1

The hot solution can be filtered into a small conical flask, but on a scale of 100mg or less, a Craig tube (Fig. 9.2) gives better recovery because it allows the crystals to be recovered without another filtration.

Figure 9.2

Filter the hot solution into a suitably sized Craig tube and cover the tube with aluminium foil while crystallization occurs. When crystallization is complete fit the matching (a close fit is essential) glass rod into the Craig tube and secure it tightly with a rubber band. Place the inverted assembly in a centrifuge tube (Fig. 9.2b) and put the centrifuge tube (and a counterbalancing tube) in a centrifuge. Centrifuge for a few minutes to force the mother liquor through the narrow gap into the centrifuge tube, and then remove the Craig tube. Tap the tube to dislodge any crystals attached to the neck, cover the tube with foil, and dry the crystals under vacuum.

If necessary the product can be recrystallized again in the same tube. Dissolve in the minimum volume of hot solvent as usual. The neck of the tube will act as a condenser but care is required, and the tube should be no more than one third full in order to avoid losses due to splashing or frothing of the refluxing solution. Cooling and centrifuging then gives another batch of crystals. This process can be carried out several times with minimal losses.

Crystallization at low temperature

Occasionally the most convenient method of purifying a low melting solid or a thermally unstable liquid may be by low temperature crystallization. This technique is attended by two important complications. First, cooling the materials and apparatus below ambient temperature will cause condensation to form. If the compound being crystallized is inert to water, and can be easily dried, then the condensation is not a major problem and normal recrystallization methods can be adopted particularly if drying tubes are used to protect the solutions. A more satisfactory solution is to carry out the crystallization under an inert atmosphere. The second difficulty is that of keeping the solutions cold during the filtration and washing steps. This can be achieved by using apparatus which can be immersed in ordinary cold baths, by using specially built apparatus with integral jackets for holding cooling solutions, or in small scale work by carrying out these steps very rapidly.

A number of ingenious solutions to these technical problems have been developed, but only a few methods which involve standard organic laboratory glassware will be described here.

For medium to large scale crystallizations ($\geq$ 1g) a set-up along the lines shown in Fig. 9.3 may be used. The compound is dissolved in the minimum volume of solvent at room temperature and is filtered into a two- or three-necked pear shaped flask. The flask is then fitted with an inert gas inlet and a thermometer adapter containing a filter stick connected to a bubbler. With the filter stick held above the solution the flask is purged with inert gas and placed in a cooling bath. It should be cooled slowly by gradual addition of the cooling agent to the solvent. When crystallization is complete the bubbler is disconnected and the filter stick is connected to an appropriately sized receiver using chemically inert tubing (Teflon). The filter stick is then lowered into the solution and the mother liquor is forced through into the receiver using inert gas pressure. The thermometer adapter will allow sufficient freedom of movement of the filter stick to pack the crystals to the bottom of the flask and drain off the mother liquor thoroughly. The crystals can then be washed by releasing the gas pressure and adding small amounts of *precooled* solvent *via* the three-way tap, using a cannula. The washings can then be removed using the filter stick as before. The cooling bath can be removed and the crystals isolated and dried in the usual way or the low temperature recrystallization can be repeated in the same flask.

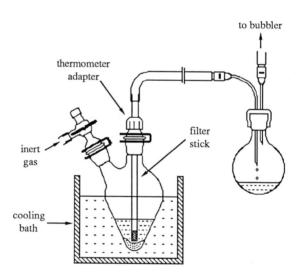

Figure 9.3

The sintered disc of the filter stick should be of porosity 3 or larger in order to avoid blockage. A convenient alternative to a filter stick is to use an ordinary glass rod with filter paper wrapped round the end (Fig. 9.4b).Wrap some Teflon tape round the end of the tube, then carefully fold filter paper over the end and secure it with wire. The Teflon tape will give a better seal because the wire will sink into it. Another alternative, which is very useful on a smaller scale, it to use a septum with an inverted needle through it (Fig. 9.4c). Again the end of the needle should be wrapped with Teflon tape and covered with filter paper, which is then secured with wire. The sharp end of the needle can be inserted into the receiving flask, thus obviating the need for connecting tubing (Fig. 9.6). These devices are also very useful for filtering reaction mixtures under an inert atmosphere, as is the filter flask described in Chapter 5 (Fig. 5.19).

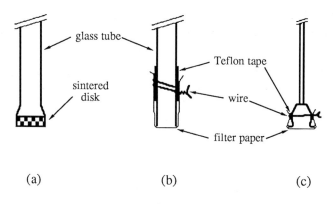

(a)   (b)   (c)

Figure 9.4

Small scale low temperature recrystallizations can be carried out in the same device recommended for ordinary small scale work. The solution is filtered into the flask and the apparatus is then purged with inert gas. The outlet is sealed with a small septum and the flask immersed in a cold bath almost up to the level of the sintered disk (Fig. 9.5).

Figure 9.5

When crystallization is complete the outlet septum is removed, the apparatus is removed from the cold bath and wiped dry, and the suspension is filtered rapidly under inert gas pressure. On a small scale the solution will not warm up significantly during the short time required to filter off the crystals. The crystals can be washed with precooled solvent in the usual way.

Crystallization of air-sensitive compounds

Clearly the recrystallization of air and moisture sensitive compounds must be carried out under an inert atmosphere. The trickiest step in this regard is often the introduction of the crude solid into the recrystallization flask. It may be possible to do this by transferring it very quickly in the air or using a "blanket" of inert gas under a funnel (Fig. 5.20). For very sensitive compounds the transfer of the solid must be carried out in a glove bag or a glove box.

Once the solid has been placed in the flask the remaining problems are similar to those described for low temperature recrystallizations under inert atmosphere. Many methods for carrying out inert atmosphere recrystallizations have been developed but organic chemists are rarely likely to need anything more sophisticated than those described in the previous section. Those methods involve inert atmosphere filtration using a filter stick (Fig. 9.3) or a flask with an integral sintered disk (Fig. 9.5) and we leave it to the reader to devize variations appropriate to his particular problem. Figure 9.6 shows a typical set-up which could be used either for filtration of the hot solution or for removal of the mother liquor from the recrystallized product.

One particular problem which arises with air sensitive materials is that they tend to be contaminated with small amounts of decomposition products which can block filters. Also if a sintered disc is used it must be scrupulously dry in order to prevent some hydrolysis occurring in the pores of the disc, which will rapidly block the filter. For these reasons the filter sticks made using filter paper are probably better than sintered discs, and at least one dry filter should be kept at hand in case the first one is blocked.

Figure 9.6

9.4.2 Distillation

Distillation is the most useful method of purifying liquids. It is used routinely for purifying solvents and reagents and, with care and the correct apparatus, it can be used to separate liquids whose boiling points are less than 5°C apart. We will assume that the reader is familiar with the fundamentals of the theory and practice of distillation but it is appropriate to begin by reiterating some basic safety rules.

1. Never heat a closed system.
2. Remember that most organic liquids are extremely flammable so great care must be taken to ensure that the vapour does not come into contact with flames, sources of sparks (electrical motors), or very hot surfaces (hot plates).
3. Never allow a distillation pot to boil dry. The residues may ignite or explode.

4. Beware of the possibility that ethers and hydrocarbons may be contaminated with peroxides (Section 4.4).
5. Carry out a safety audit on the compound you plan to distil to check that it is not thermally unstable. Some types of compounds, e.g. azides, should never be distilled.

Simple distillation

The conventional apparatus for simple distillation is shown in Fig. 9.7. It is only useful for distilling compounds from involatile residues, or for separating liquids whose boiling points differ by at least 50°C. Moisture can be excluded by attaching a drying tube to the vent or by connecting the vent to an inert gas line. It is essential to add some boiling chips, or better to stir the liquid, in order to prevent bumping, especially if a finely divided solid, such as a drying agent, is present.

thermometer
thermometer adapter
stillhead
condenser
receiver adapter
stirring bar

Figure 9.7

The flask should be heated in a water bath, or an oil bath, ***not*** with a Bunsen burner or a heating mantle (Section 8.4.2). The temperature of the bath should be increased slowly until distillation begins and then it should be adjusted to give a steady rate of distillation. If the boiling point is high

(>150°C) the stillhead may need to be lagged with glass wool, and an air condenser should be used rather than a water condenser.

For routine solvent distillation it is more convenient to use a compact distillation apparatus such as that shown in Fig. 9.8. These can be bought, or constructed in two or three convenient sizes to fit the common ground glass joints.

solid
glass rod

Figure 9.8

If the distillation is being used to dry a reagent, the process must be carried out under an inert atmosphere. To do this, first of all dry all glass apparatus in an oven, or with a heat gun under vacuum, and purge with argon whilst cooling. This is most easily accomplished by connecting the apparatus to a double manifold/bubbler system (see Chapter 3). Although Quickfit assemblies can be used, we prefer one piece type distillation apparatus, as shown in Fig. 9.8 and Fig. 9.9b. When the glassware has cooled, increase the argon flow, quickly disconnect the distillation flask, add any drying agent required, a few anti-bumping granules, and the liquid to be distilled, and reassemble the system. Heat the distillation flask *in an oil bath* (do not carry out distillations using a heating mantle) and collect the distillate which comes over at the required temperature. When the distillation is complete remove the collector and seal it quickly with a septum. Most reagents can simply be poured into a reagent bottle before sealing, provided you are quick. However, if the reagent is particularly sensitive to air or moisture a cannulation technique should be used to transfer it (see Chapter 5). Whatever type of container is used for storage it is always preferable that it be full or nearly so.

(a)   (b)   (c)

Figure   9.9

Fractional distillation

Separation of liquids whose boiling points are between 5°C and 50°C apart
requires the use of an apparatus which gives better contact between the
vapour and liquid phases in the distillation column. Columns which do this
are called fractionating columns and the most common type, a Vigreux
column, is shown in Fig. 9.9. A 50cm long vacuum jacketed Vigreux (Fig.
9.9a) should allow reasonable separation of compounds which boil 30-40°C
apart. The Vigreux assembly shown in Fig. 9.9b is less efficient but is
convenient for routine distillations and gives quite good results at reduced
pressure. The keys to getting good results from a fractional distillation are
to raise the temperature very gradually, and to collect the distillate very
slowly.

Efficient separation of compounds with a boiling point difference of 10-
30°C can be achieved using a long glass tube packed with glass rings or
helices, or for high efficiency, wire mesh rings (Fig. 9.9c). A description
of the technique for operating such columns is beyond the scope of this

book. Two more sophisticated commercially available designs are the 'Spaltrohr' columns which consist of concentric grooved tubes, and spinning band columns in which a rapidly spinning spiral band is fitted inside the column. Both of these systems have low hold ups and give very high efficiency so they can be used for the separation of small volumes (as little as 1ml) and for separating compounds with very similar boiling points (as little as 3°C). Consult the manufacturer's manuals for operating instructions for these devices.

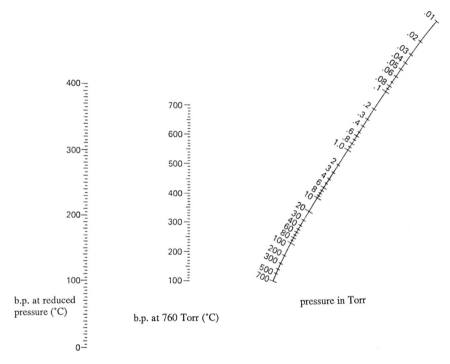

Figure 9.10

Distillation under reduced pressure

Many compounds decompose when heated to their boiling points so they cannot be distilled at atmospheric pressure. In this situation it may be possible to avoid thermal decomposition by carrying out the distillation at reduced pressure. The reduction in the boiling point will depend on the reduction in pressure and it can be estimated from a pressure-temperature nomograph (Fig. 9.10). To find the *approximate* boiling point at any pressure simply place a ruler on the central line at the atmospheric boiling point of the compound, pivot it to line up with the appropriate pressure marking on the right-hand line, and read off the predicted boiling point from the left-hand line. You can also use the nomograph to find the b.p. at any pressure if you know the b.p. at some other pressure, by first using the known data to arrive at an estimate of the atmospheric boiling point. Note that although pressure is usually measured in millimetres of mercury (mmHg) it is often quoted in different units, especially Torr. Happily 1 Torr = 1mmHg. Boiling points measured at reduced pressure may be expressed in several ways, e.g. 57°C/25mmHg or b.p.$_{25}$ 57°C. As a very rough guide a water pump (ca. 15mmHg) will give a 125°C reduction in boiling point and an oil pump (ca. 0.1mmHg) will give a reduction of 200-250°C. A typical vacuum distillation apparatus is shown in Fig. 9.11.

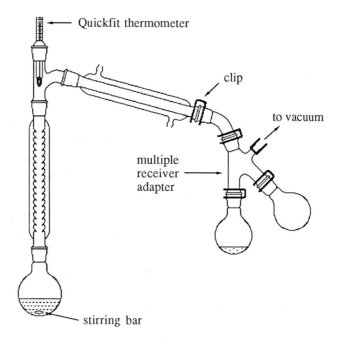

Figure 9.11

The chief difference from the simple distillation apparatus is in the design of the receiver adaptor. This must allow several fractions to be collected without needing to break the vacuum. The simplest design is the 'pig' type shown in Fig. 9.12a. When using a pig, remember to grease the joint lightly so that the receiver can be rotated while under vacuum, and to fix the receivers securely using clips.

(a)   (b)

Figure 9.12

The procedure for carrying out the distillation is as follows.

1. Place the sample in the distillation flask (no more than two thirds full) and add a stirring bar. Anti-bumping granules are not effective at reduced pressure and so an alternative must be used. A very narrow capillary which allows a slow stream of air or nitrogen bubbles to pass through the solution is effective, but brisk stirring using a magnetic follower is much more convenient.

2. Assemble the (oven-dried) apparatus, putting a little high vacuum grease on each joint. Ensure that the receiver adapter and the collection flasks are secured using clips, and connect the assembly to a vacuum pump. One convenient method of doing this is to connect it to a vacuum/inert gas double manifold (Chapter 3). The pump must be protected with a cold finger trap and the line should contain a gauge for monitoring the pressure (Chapter 7).

3. Stir the liquid rapidly and carefully open the apparatus to the vacuum. Some bumping and frothing may occur as air and volatile components are evacuated. Adjust the pressure to the required value by allowing inert gas into the system *via* a needle valve.

4. Heat the flask slowly to drive off any volatile impurities and then to distil the product. Monitor the stillhead temperature and collect a forerun and a main fraction, which should distil at a fairly constant temperature. If fractionation is required you may have to collect several fractions and it is very important to distil the mixture slowly and steadily.

5. Stop the distillation when the level of liquid in the pot is running low, by removing the heating bath.

6. Isolate the apparatus from the vacuum and carefully fill with inert gas. The flask containing the distillate is now under a dry, inert atmosphere and should be quickly removed and fitted with a tightly fitting septum .

7. Switch off the pump and clean the cold trap.

A Perkin triangle (Fig. 9.12b) is a more convenient device for collecting fractions on a larger scale. It is operated as follows.

1. Attach a receiver and open both the apparatus and the receiver to the vacuum using taps A and B. Open tap C and collect the forerun in the receiver.

2. Close tap C so that the next fraction will collect in the bulb D, while you are removing the receiver. Use tap B to allow inert gas/air into the receiver, and then replace the receiver with a new one.

3. Close tap A to temporarily isolate the still. Evacuate the receiver by opening tap B to the vacuum. Wait until the pressure has steadied, open tap A, and then open tap C to allow the distillate to drain into the new receiver.

4. Continue to collect fractions by repeating steps 3 and 4 as necessary.

Small scale distillation

The chief difficulty with small scale distillations is that a significant proportion of the sample may be lost in 'wetting' the surface of the column and the condenser. This problem is reduced by using very compact designs, but this reduces the efficiency of the columns thus making fractionation impractical. Different apparatus designs, giving different tradeoffs between recovery and efficiency, are available. A typical example, featuring a short Vigreux and a rotary fraction collector, is shown in Fig. 9.13. Very small quantities can be distilled in a cold-finger sublimation apparatus (Fig. 9.15). Spinning band and Spaltrohr columns combine high efficiency with low hold up so they provide an effective, if expensive, solution to the problem of fractionation of small volumes (> 1ml).

to vacuum

multiple fraction collector

stirring bar

Figure 9.13

Another popular solution to these problems is the Buchi Kugelrohr apparatus (Fig. 9.14). The key features of this system are (i) a horizontal oven (made of glass or metal) with an iris closure, which heats the flasks efficiently, (ii) short path distillation between a series of bulbs which can be moved horizontally in and out of the oven, and (iii) a motor to rotate the bulbs (optional). The Kugelrohr can be used to distil very small quantities (< 100mg) and can be operated at high vacuum. A simple distillation is carried out as follows. Place the sample in the end bulb using a Pasteur pipette. If necessary wash the sample into the bulb and then evaporate the solvent on a rotary evaporator. Add two more bulbs and a straight length of tubing, insert the tube in the motor assembly, and slide the end bulb into the oven. Gently close the iris type seal gently onto the connecting joint. Set the bulbs rotating (to prevent bumping and speed up the distillation), apply the vacuum and raise the oven temperature gradually. When distillation is complete allow the flasks to cool under an inert atmosphere and then remove the bulbs from the apparatus and recover the distillate. Fractionation of compounds with a 20-30°C boiling point difference can be achieved by inserting all the bulbs except one into the oven, distilling the most volatile component into that bulb, withdrawing the next bulb from the oven and distilling the next fraction into that, and so on.

Figure 9.14

9.4.3 Sublimation

Sublimation is an excellent method for purifying relatively volatile organic solids on scales ranging from a few milligrams to tens of grams. At reduced pressure many compounds, especially those of low polarity, have a sufficiently high vapour pressure that they can be sublimed, i.e. converted directly from the solid phase into the vapour phase without melting. Condensation of the vapour then gives purified solid product provided, as is often the case, that the original impurities were much less volatile. Two designs of sublimation apparatus are shown in Fig. 9.15. The larger sublimator (Fig. 9.15a) consists of a tube with a side arm which is fitted with a cold-finger condenser. It is used as follows. If the crude material is a solid, powder it and place it in the bottom of the outer vessel. If it is waxy or oily, wash it into the tube with a *small amount* of solvent, cover the side arm with a septum, and remove the solvent on a rotary evaporator. Put some vacuum grease on the joint of the cold-finger condenser and fit it into the sublimator (there should be a gap of approximately 1cm between the solid and the condenser). Evacuate the apparatus slowly to try to prevent any spattering of the solid. Turn on the condenser water and slowly heat the base of the sublimator. A fine mist of sublimed material on the condenser indicates that sublimation is beginning and the temperature should then be held fairly constant until the process is complete. At this stage the sublimed product may be clinging precariously to the cold finger so proceed with great care. Turn off the water, *carefully* allow air/inert gas into the sublimator, and *very carefully* remove the cold-finger. Scrape off the product with a microspatula.

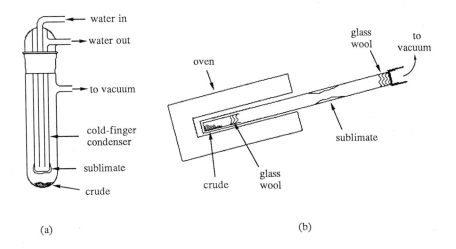

Figure 9.15

The simple glass tube shown in Fig. 9.15b functions in a similar way except that the water condenser is omitted. Place the crude sample in a small sample vial, put a plug of glass wool in the neck, and drop the vial into the tube. Put a plug of glass wool in the neck of the tube and attach it to a vacuum line. Evacuate carefully and heat the base of the tube gently in an oil bath or in a custom designed metal block as shown. Proceed as before and isolate the sublimed product by cutting the tube and scraping out the solid.

9.5   Chromatographic purification of reaction products

Chromatographic techniques for analysis and purification of reaction products are probably the most universally important of all the skills in which an organic chemist requires expertise!

Before attempting any of the chromatographic separation techniques described in this section you will need to be confident about your ability in running analytical tlc (see Chapter 8), as the two skills are very closely interlinked. For routine separation and purification of reaction products, some form of column chromatography is normally employed. Traditionally long columns were filled with silica and a good head of solvent was used, so that a flow was achieved by force of gravity. This method of chromatography is very slow and the slow elution rate not only wastes time, but also but leads to band dispersion. This *reduces* the resolution and often leads to a large number of fractions which contain a mixture of compounds. The technique has therefore become obsolete, and has been largely superseded by flash chromatography.

9.5.1 Flash chromatography

Flash chromatography was introduced by Still, Khan and Mitra in 1978[1]. It has cut down the time taken for routine purification of reaction mixtures considerably and, perhaps more importantly, has provided the chemist with a fast and simple technique for separating isomeric materials which have similar polarities. It has become the standard method of purification in many synthetic laboratories, with a resultant reduction in the time taken to achieve many synthetic goals.

The key to the effectiveness of flash chromatography is that a comparatively fine silica powder is used, with a relatively narrow particle range (e.g. Merck C60, 40-63μm, type 9385 or May and Baker Sorbsil C60 40-60μm). This silica gives better surface contact, and therefore more effective adsorption, than that previously used for gravity columns. The pressure required to drive the solvent through increases the resolution by cutting down band dispersion and considerably reduces the time required for running the column.

There are some practical difficulties with the original published method

1. W.C. Still, M. Khan and, A. Mitra, *J. Org. Chem.*, 1978 **43**, 2923

for running flash columns and modifications have therefore been introduced over the years. These make the technique easier to carry out and somewhat safer. This section will lead you through the basic steps for running a modified version of flash chromatography which we find to be very convenient and effective. Flash chromatography is a very powerful and rapid technique for separation of organic compounds, but like all chromatographic techniques *you will only gain expertise by experience,* and these instructions can only be considered as guide-lines. Every separation is different so do not be despondent if you have some failures at first. With practice you should be able to acquire the skill and intuition required to get good separation, even in the most difficult circumstances, every time, *and quickly!*

Equipment required

The set-up originally described by Still requires the use of long columns, to accommodate a reasonable supply of solvent, but these are difficult to load and need to be dismantled for addition of extra solvent during the run. We therefore recommend the use of shorter columns plus a reservoir. It is important to have a familiar set of columns on hand and we suggest that you have a set of about five columns, ranging in diameter from about 5mm to 50mm. A very convenient length for all columns is 25cm, except for those with a very narrow bore, which can be shorter (Fig. 9.16). It is convenient to standardize on a B24 (24/40) joint on the top of the column and a glassblower can make reservoirs from a round-bottom flask and a male joint. The 250ml reservoir is used more than any other, but it is also useful to have 100ml, 500ml, and 1 litre sizes available.

We find that it is difficult to control the column pressure using a Rotaflow valve as suggested in the original paper and this can be dangerous if too much pressure is inadvertently applied. Two alternative methods are used successfully in our labs. One of these is simply to use a rubber bellows attached directly to a tubing inlet and apply enough pressure to give the required flow rate. The only problem with this technique is that it is difficult to keep the pressure constant, particularly with large columns. An alternative is to construct a simple pressure-release valve, such as that shown in Fig. 9.17 and use this in conjunction with a compressed air supply or nitrogen cylinder.

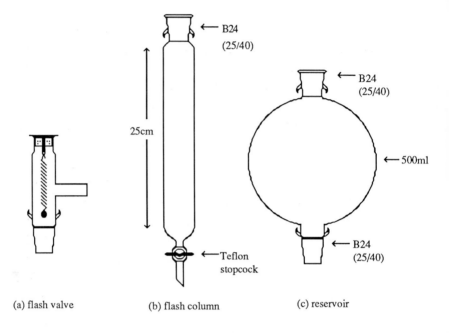

(a) flash valve   (b) flash column   (c) reservoir

Figure 9.16

The glass part of the 'flash adapter' is made from a B24 joint and a piece of 14mm i.d. heavy wall tubing. The valve is simply a septum, with the skirt cut off, glued to a shaped metal (brass) plate.

Constuction of 'flash valve'

Figure 9.17

The adapter should be constructed with the dimensions shown and fitted with standard 4cm stainless steel lab springs and it will then provide a constant, safe pressure, which will give a suitable flow rate for all purposes. It is also possible to use a small compressor, such as a fish tank pump, or small diaphragn pump, to provide a suitable pressure source.

For analysis of the column fractions, have a tlc tank close at hand containing an appropriate solvent, and several tlc plates, cut to about 4cm wide.

For relatively small columns the most suitable way for collecting fractions is in a rack of tubes and the best type of racks are those which hold the tubes very close together (for example those supplied by Gilson/Anachem for their fraction collectors). Using this type of rack, the column flow can be changed from one tube to the next simply by moving the whole rack. For large columns, conical flasks are often more convenient for collecting fractions.

Procedure for running a flash column

Safety note:

Silica dust is very toxic if inhaled, you should therefore take precautions to avoid breathing it in and always handle it in a fume cupboard. Large volumes of solvent are also used for chromatography and you should take precautions to avoid breathing in the vapours or exposing them to sparks.

1.   Decide on the solvent system and on the quantity of silica

i)   Run tlcs to find a solvent system which will give a good separation of the components of the mixture, and a R_f value of ca. 0.2-0.3 (usually start with ethyl acetate - petroleum ether mixtures). If spots are running close together an R_f value of 0.2-0.3 at the mid-point is normally satisfactory, but if they are well separated, a solvent which puts the lower spot at R_f 0.2-0.3 will usually work. If you know which spot you are most interested in, try to bias your judgement towards this. There are often irrelevant impurities which are either very polar or very non-polar and these can be largely ignored.

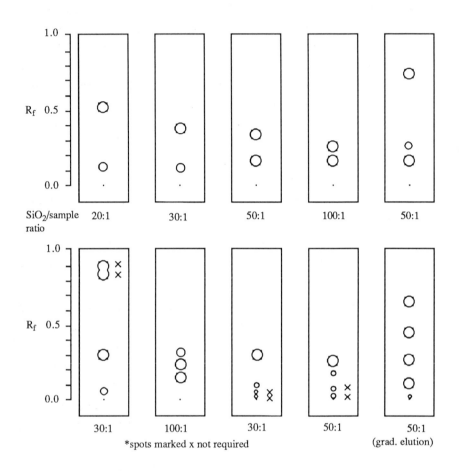

Figure 9.18

ii)   You should try to use as little silica as possible since it is quite
      expensive. Where the component you require is well separated from
      other components, a ratio of ca. 20:1 (silica:mixture) should be
      sufficient. For more difficult separations up to 100:1 ratio can be used
      (with a ratio of 100:1 spots that are touching on tlc should be separable
      in the appropriate solvent system). As a rough guide some
      representations of tlcs are given in Fig. 9.18 which indicate a solvent
      system which could be selected for separation of the mixture. Below
      the drawings, an approximation of the relative quantity of silica
      (compared to the sample) required to bring about separation is given.

An important fact to remember for all chromatographic separations is that the more spots there are in the mixture, the greater the ratio of silica for each individual separation. Thus, you normally require *less* not more silica to separate a 3 spot mixture, than for a 2 spot mixture having similar separations. It is in this first step of the procedure that the greatest skill and judgement is required and careful attention should be paid to trial tlc's. With experience, the appropriate column and solvent to choose will become almost instinctive.

2. Choose and prepare the column

i) Weigh out the required quantity of silica in a conical flask and make it into a mobile slurry with some of the chosen solvent.

ii) Choose a column which will fill to about 18cm with the amount of silica being used (it is useful to mark columns once you know how much they hold).

iii) To plug the bottom of the column: roll a piece of cotton wool between the fingers so that it is just wider than the column outlet; connect the column to a low vacuum line with the tap closed; drop the cotton wool ball to the bottom of the column, then open the tap. This is the most reliable way to insert the plug.

iv) Mount the column vertically using a clamp stand, pour about 8cm of the solvent in and then carefully sprinkle a layer of fine sand (ca. 1mm), to cover the plug.

v) *Very carefully* add the silica slurry to the column, in small portions, *via* a powder funnel. Between each portion, pressurize the column to pack down the silica and remove excess solvent. *Be careful not to allow the the solvent to drop below the level of the top of the silica.*

vi) When all the silica has been loaded, leave a good head of solvent on top of it and sprinkle in enough sand to cover the surface of the silica evenly (ca. 1mm). Then force the excess solvent through the column until there is just a small layer left above the sand. There should now be a *flat* layer of silica covered by a thin and even layer of sand.

air or
nitrogen

rubber bands

Alternative inlet for
attachment to bellows
or low pressure pump

rubber bands

sand

pasteur
pipette

cotton wool

sand

(a) loading the column   (b) complete column set-up

Figure 9.19

Note:

The column once prepared can be left for a *very short* time, but once
you load the sample the remaining steps should be carried out as swiftly
as possible, and the solvent flow should be continued without
interruption if possible, especially during the early stages of elution.

Leaving the column standing with the sample loaded leads to band dispersion and loss of resolution. So, before starting the remainder of the procedure make sure you have everything that you will need to hand, including plenty of solvent.

3. *Load the sample*

i)   Dissolve the sample in the minimum amount of solvent, preferably the same solvent that you intend to run the column in (if this is not possible as is often the case, dissolve the sample in a small amount of dichloromethane)†. Keep a tlc sample of the sample mixture to compare with the column fractions.

ii) Load the solution onto the top of the column, *very carefully*, using a Pasteur pipette to drip it around the walls of the column, just above the sand. Caution must be taken not to disturb the layer of sand. Repeat the procedure using the minimum quantity of solvent to rinse any remaining sample from the flask.

iii) Once all the solution has been added allow the level of liquid to drop so that the top of the sand is just starting to dry.

4. *Add the solvent*

i)   Add the solvent to the top of the column, *very carefully* at first, again using a Pasteur pipette to drip solvent around the walls of the column just above the sand, and taking care not to disturb the sand. Once a head of solvent is present, more can be poured in *carefully* from a beaker.

ii) Attach a solvent reservoir to the top of the column, secure it with elastic bands (Bibby clips are not strong enough), and fill with solvent.

5. *Run the column*

i)   Connect bellows or flash adapter to the top of the reservoir and secure with elastic bands (your set-up should then look like the diagram shown in Fig. 9.19).†

ii) Apply pressure to give a fast solvent flow rate and collect fractions continuously. It is very important to maintain a fast flow rate through

---

†   For some very non-polar compounds, even small quantities of methylene chloride may cause elution problems and an alternative method of loading can be used. Thus, a solution of the sample is added to a small amount of silica in a round bottom flask and the mixture is evaporated to dryness. The dry impregnated silica is then added to the top of the pre-packed column.

the column - the solvent should run, rather than drip! *A slow flow rate causes reduced resolution, NOT improved separation.*[††] The size of fractions will depend mainly upon the size of the column and as a rough guide, they should be in ml about half the weight of silica (i.e. for a 30g column you should collect ca.15ml fractions). It is a myth that you get less mixtures by collecting smaller fractions - the mixture simply appears in more tubes and leads to a good deal of extra work! You may feel safer collecting relatively small fractions at first, but as you become more experienced you will tend to collect larger fractions, and thus considerably lower the amount of time you spend on chromatography. *Always be careful not to let the column run dry.*

iii) Monitor the column fractions by running tlcs whilst the column is running (5 or 6 spots per tlc plate is usually a convenient amount). You should have time to apply a spot of the previous fraction to a tlc plate whilst the present fraction is collecting.

6. *Analyse tlcs and combine fractions*

    When all the compounds you are interested in have eluted, and you have identified in which fractions they are, combine the fractions as appropriate (keeping fractions that contain mixtures separate from those containing pure materials). Remove the solvent from the combined fractions on a rotary evaporator, and finally remove the last traces of solvent under high vacuum.

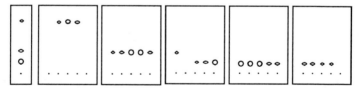

Figure 9.20 Typical set of tlcs for a successful column

Gradient elution

When the components of a mixture run close together, a single solvent system which gives the spots a tlc R_f of 0.2-0.3, will be effective. However, when the spots are a long way apart, increasing the solvent

---

[††] A pressure of 7psi is recommended in Still's original paper, but we tend to rely on flow rate, rather than pressure.

polarity as the column is running will save a good deal of time and solvent - this is referred to as gradient elution. You should be confident with single solvent chromatography before you attempt gradient elution, as it requires quite a bit of experienced judgement. The procedure for doing this is:

1. Start running the column in a solvent which will give the highest running spot an R_f of 0.2-0.3.
2. When tlc analysis indicates that this component is almost completely off, change the solvent polarity to that which gives the second spot an R_f of 0.3. In some cases you may need to change the solvent polarity in steps.
3. Continue this process until all the spots that you require are off.

Recycling procedure for flash silica

Flash silica is quite expensive but if you can buy it in bulk (25kg at a time) the cost will be reduced by nearly half. Another way to save money is to recycle it, using the procedure given below. The material generated by this method is very reliable.

1. *Washing*

   Suspend 1kg of silica in 1.5 litres of acetone, stir, then filter on a Buchner funnel and wash with an additional 1 litre of acetone, followed by 2 litres of deionized water

2. *Ignition*

   Place the silica in a large crucible and dry at 120-140°C overnight. Then heat in a muffle furnace at 500-600°C for 4h.

3. *Coarse particle removal*

   After cooling, place the silica in a bucket containing about 5 litres of deionized water. Mix the suspension thoroughly, avoiding vortexing, and allow the mixture to settle for 30 s. Then *carefully* pour the top 50% of the mixture into a second bucket. Make the first bucket up to 5 litres, stir again, allow to settle for 30 s and again decant off the first 50% into the second bucket. Repeat this procedure twice further then discard the remaining contents of the first bucket.

4 . Fine particle removal

The second bucket should now contain about 10 litres of silica/water mixture. Stir this thoroughly and allow it to settle for 4 min. Decant off the first 50% *carefully* and discard it. Stir again, then allow to settle for 4 min, decant off the first 50% and discard again. Repeat this procedure twice more, after making up to 5 litres each time.

5 . Activation

Filter the silica in a Buchner funnel then dry in an oven at 120-130°C overnight. Recovery should be 650-800g.

9.5.2 Dry-column flash chromatography

This technique was developed by Harwood[2] and can be used as an alternative to flash chromatography. The apparatus simply consists of a parallel-sided vacuum filter funnel, incorporating a porosity 3 sinter (see Chapter 3) and a flask (Fig. 9.21).

Figure 9.21

Method for running the column

1 . Column packing

Fill the funnel to the lip with tlc grade silica (e.g. Merck Kieselgel 60) and tap gently, then apply suction from a water aspirator, pressing the silica down starting at the circumference and working towards the centre. Continue until a level and firm bed is obtained and there is a head space for

---

2. L.M. Harwood, *Aldrichimica Acta*, 1985, **18**, 25

sample and solvent addition. The approximate funnel sizes, compared with the quantity of sample to be applied, are given in Table 9.1.

Table 9.1

Funnel Diameter(mm)	Funnel Length(mm)	Weight of Silica(g)	Weight of Sample(mg)	Fraction Size(ml)
30	45	15	15-500	10-15
40	50	30	500-2000	15-30
70	55	100	1000-5000	20-50

2. Pre-elution

Under vacuum, pre-elute the column with a solvent which will give a tlc R_f of about 0.2 for the least polar constituent of the sample. If the silica has been packed correctly, the solvent should run down the column with a horizontal front, but if it channels, the column should be sucked dry and re-packed. Keep the surface of the silica covered with solvent while pre-eluting until solvent starts collecting, then suck it dry.

3. Loading the sample

Load the sample as a solution, in the same solvent as used for pre-elution, in an even layer onto the surface of the silica. Alternatively, if the sample is insoluble in the pre-elution solvent, it can be pre-adsorbed onto a small quantity of silica (see Section 9.5.1, loading a flash column)) which is then spread on the surface of the silica in the funnel.

4. Eluting the column

Sequentially add solvent fractions to the funnel according to the quantities indicated in Table 9.1, sucking the silica dry in between each fraction, and keeping fractions separate. For each successive fraction increase the solvent polarity by increasing the proportion of the more polar solvent by about 5-10% (e.g. from 50% EtOAc/50% petrol to 55% EtOAc, for a 10% increase). Analyse the fractions by tlc to determine the locations of the components of interest, but as a rough guide, the solvent mixture which would give the compound a tlc R_f value of about 0.5 will probably elute it.

As with any chromatographic technique expertise will only come with experience, but given that, you should be able to separate quite closely running compounds quickly using this technique.

9.5.3 Preparative tlc

Until quite recently preparative tlc was widely used for separating small quantities of compounds of similar polarity, but the technique has largely been superseded by the development of flash chromatography and hplc, each of which can give better resolution. Thickly coated 'prep plates' should definitely be considered a thing of the past, but some people still do like to run large (e.g. 20 x 10cm) analytical plates as prep plates, and about 10mg can be loaded onto this size plate.

A high degree of skill is required to draw a tlc dropper across a line at the base of the plate, applying a very thin and even line of the sample solution, without damaging the silica. In between each application the solvent is allowed to dry before a further application is made, and this process is repeated until all the sample has been loaded.

After running the plate (multiple elution is often required for good separation), it is viewed under a uv lamp and the bands are marked with a fine pencil (it is very difficult to use prep tlc for non-uv active compounds). A sharp scalpel is used to cut the bands and scrape them carefully off the plate and the compound is separated from the silica by washing through a cotton-wool plug with a very small quantity of methanol. After evaporation it is necessary to re-dissolve the compound in methylene chloride and filter again to remove traces of silica.

Great skill is required to run preparative tlcs effectively, and even then the sample obtained is often contaminated with significant quantities of grease and tlc plate binding agent. Since there are now much better modern small scale separation techniques available, we do not recommend preparative tlc (see below for details of preparative hplc and Chapter 10 for more on small scale flash chromatography).

9.5.4 Medium pressure liquid chromatography (mplc)

There are often times when quite difficult separations need to be performed on a fairly large scale. Even if the mixture will separate by flash chromatography, it may be prohibitively expensive, especially if it is a step which needs to be carried out routinely. This is one occasion when mplc is very useful. The resolution of mplc is somewhat better than flash chromatography, but another important feature is that the columns are reused many times, thus avoiding the expense of throwing away large quantities of silica.

Setting up an mplc system

Figure 9.22

The mplc system is essentially a simplified and much cheaper version of an hplc set-up. At the heart of the system is any type of pump which will operate at 100psi, with a controllable flow rate of up to 100ml/min. There are a variety of moderately-priced pumps on the market, including one produced by Buchi, which is especially designed for mplc. However, we use a Gilson hplc pump, which has interchangeable flow heads. For mplc, a 100ml head is fitted, but the same pump can also be used for either analytical or preparative hplc, simply by changing the head. Since glass columns are used for mplc it is important that a pressure limiting valve is fitted in-line, to prevent high pressure building up in the column, in the event of a blockage. The valve should normally be set to cut off the pump at about 100psi, but you should consult the instructions for your columns before setting this.

All the pipework used in the mplc system is 3mm Teflon tubing, which is very easily tailored to your needs. The tubing is connected to the various components of the system by plastic screw ferules, which should only be tightened finger tight. It is very easy to make up the tubing to suit your needs, but you will need a flanging tool to fit the ferules onto the tube ends (Fig. 9.23). The tubing can be connected using threaded plastic sleeves (Fig. 9.24).

Figure 9.23 Fitting a ferule to 3mm teflon tubing

Figure 9.24 Connecting 3mm tubing using a threaded sleeve

The sample is introduced into the system *via* an injection valve, but this is a much simpler and less expensive valve than that found in an hplc system. We use a Rheodyne type 50 Teflon rotary valve, which will take a flow rate of 100ml/min (Fig. 9.25). The pump and the column are connected to the red and white connectors respectively, whilst a sample load loop (see below) is fitted to the black and yellow connectors. A Luer fitting is attached to the blue connector, which is where the sample is introduced, using a syringe. The green connector is a vent and should be positioned so that effluent from it can be collected in a beaker or flask.

side view

Figure 9.25 Rheodyne Type 50 mplc injection valve

In the 'load' mode (anti-clockwise position), solvent from the pump inlet (red) passes directly out into the column (white). In this mode the sample inlet (blue) is connected through the load loop (black and yellow) to the vent (green). Thus with the solvent flow by-passing the load loop, sample can be injected from a syringe onto the loop, displacing any residual solvent out of the vent.

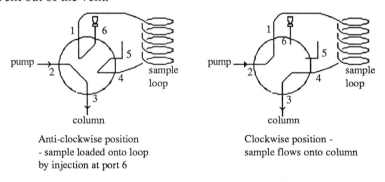

Anti-clockwise position
- sample loaded onto loop
by injection at port 6

Clockwise position -
sample flows onto column

Figure 9.26 Flow through mplc injection valve

On switching the valve clockwise to the alternative 'inject' position, the solvent stream is diverted through the load loop, introducing the sample onto the column (Fig. 9.26).

Load loops are made very simply by coiling a length of 3mm Teflon tubing which holds the required volume and fitting ferules on either end - 10, 25 and 50 ml loops are useful sizes to make.

There are now several manufacturers of good quality glass mplc columns. The ones we use are made by Buchi and we have found them to be very effective. They are available in a wide variety of sizes and it is convenient to have a selection, but if your budget is tight, just one large column would be very useful. The column we use most frequently is 50cm long by 50mm wide and we can separate between 8 and 20g on this depending on the separation. It is useful to have a small 'scrubber' column in front of the main column, which will prolong its useful life. Each column manufacturer will recommend a packing method, and Buchi supply a special loader for their columns, which is very quick and simple to use, and packs the silica dry under compressed air pressure.

There is a choice of silica available for mplc, but for most purposes ordinary 'flash' (40-60μm) silica is used. It is surprising to find out how much more effective this silica is under mplc conditions than under simple flash conditions. A column packed with 15-20μm silica is more effective for difficult separations but there is a lot to be said for sticking to only one, or perhaps two types of silica and becoming familiar with their characteristics. In most cases getting a good separation is simply a matter of choosing the appropriate size of column and the correct solvent. Other solid phases can also be used on an mplc system alumina, ion exchange resin, Sephadex.

The final piece of equipment which is more or less essential to an mplc system is a fraction collector. Any kind of fraction collector will work, but we use a Gilson computer controlled device, which is ideal for a variety of purposes. For small scale work we collect 20 ml fractions (Gilson number 22 rack), and for large scale we collect 60 ml fractions (sintillation rack number 24 with home-made tubes to fit).

A uv or refractive index detector can also be incorporated into the system, or the fractions can simply be analysed by tlc, as for flash chromatography. If the conditions are kept constant the results from mplc are very consistent, so if you wish to repeat separations of the same mixture, it is very easy to predict which fractions will contain each component.

Procedure for using mplc

You will normally have had experience of flash chromatography before attempting mplc, and the two are really quite similar except that the relationship between tlc polarity and column solvent is slightly different. Again there is no substitute for experience! The following list will guide you through the essential steps.

1. Decide on column and solvent

A solvent which gives an R_f between 0.2-0.4 usually works best, and the size of the column will depend on quantity and separation. As a guide, we routinely resolve 8g quantities of a quite closely running mixture on a 50 x 5cm column, but we have separated up to 20g if the separation is very good. It is always best to rely on experience and for this reason we keep a log of all the runs on the system, which includes tlc sketches, quantities, solvent system, flow rate, column information and comments. Then when you are running something for the first time, you can look back to find similar mixtures which have been separated before and gain some idea of what to use for your sample.

2. Set up the system

Set the system up as described above, re-charging the scrubber column, if one is fitted, and switch on to run solvent through the column. If the column is newly packed, recycle the effluent from the column back into the solvent reservoir and leave the instrument to equilibrate for at least 15 min. If the column already contains solvent, flush this off before recycling. *Also, set the injection valve so that solvent flows through the load loop and flushes away any solvent which was in there!* The optimum flow rate is dependent on column diameter, but will also vary with solvent , separation etc. The following figures are a rough guide: about 20ml/min for a 25mm column; about 45ml/min for a 35mm column; 75-85ml/min for a 50mm column and 100ml/min for anything larger (see under preparative hplc for flow rate calculation). Having chosen the flow rate, set the fraction collector to stop at each tube for an appropriate time.

3. Sample preparation

Mplc is a separation technique and not a clean-up technique, and since the columns are re-used, any base-line material or inorganic solid should be removed from the sample before you start. This can be done either by simple filtration or by filtration through a small pad of silica in a short column. While the mplc column is equilibrating, make up a concentrated solution of the sample in either the chosen solvent or in methylene chloride.

4. *Load the sample*

Switch the injection valve to the 'load' position (Fig. 9.26, solvent by-passing the loop). Using a good syringe with a flat-ended needle, draw up the sample, then invert the syringe and hold it with the needle pointing upwards. Next draw in an air bubble of about 1ml and remove the needle from the syringe. Still holding the syringe in the inverted position, *carefully connect it to the Luer fitting* on the injection valve. Now turn the syringe the right way up and inject the sample until all the solution and a very small bubble have entered the load loop. To avoid a sudden pressure build-up as the sample is injected, reduce the flow rate by half, then switch the injection valve *quickly*. As the sample begins to enter the column, gradually turn the flow rate back up and start the fraction collector.

5. *Running the column*

Whilst the column is running, collect tlcs or use the detector to determine which fractions contain the required components. Unless you are using a refractive index detector, gradient elution is simply achieved by gradually adding more polar solvent to the reservoir.

6. *Finishing the run*

Before you leave the system make sure all the components that were loaded onto the column have been eluted and if necessary, run a more polar solvent through to remove polar material. The column can be left with a length of Teflon tubing attached between the ends to prevent it drying out.

7. *Regenerating columns*

Sometimes a column will become contaminated with stubborn polar material. 'Back-washing' some columns is possible, but this is not necessarily the best way to treat them. It is better to run a polar solvent through, such as methanol (or even water), then gradually change the solvent back to a less polar system, through the sequence: water; methanol; ethyl acetate; ethyl acetate/petrol; petrol.

9.5.5 Preparative hplc

Equipment required

A preparative hplc system has exactly the same components as an analytical system, except that several features are larger (see Chapter 8). With some systems, such as the Gilson, the pump head can simply be changed to provide the higher flow rates required. The injection valve must also be the large bore type (e.g. Rheodyne 7125) fitted with a large load loop (up to 5ml), and of course the columns are much larger. It is also useful, but not essential, to have a fraction collector, and if this is microprocessor controlled, it can be liked to the detector so that fractions are only collected when a peak is being detected. There are now several extremely sophisticated, computer-controlled systems available, which can be set to inject samples automatically and collect selected peaks into designated flasks. Thus, large quantities of material can be separated over multiple injections. However, for most research purposes the prime requirement is for one-off separations.

The choice of detector can be quite critical. Uv detectors are very sensitive but are of little use if molecules without chromophores are being separated. A refractive index detector is universally applicable but has the drawback that gradient elution is virtually impossible.

Running a preparative hplc column

The sequence of events for running a preparative hplc column is almost the same as that for mplc, as described above. However, there are a few significant differences which should be taken into account, and will be described here.

Care of hplc columns

First of all you should appreciate that preparative *hplc should only be used for separation of clean mixtures*. Some other form of chromatography should always have been carried out previously to remove any material which is significantly more polar than the compounds to be separated and any suspended solid should also be removed. Preparative hplc is a very powerful technique and it is often possible to separate compounds which do not separate on tlc. However, preparative hplc columns are extremely expensive, and although they should last for a very long time, they can easily be ruined by one thoughtless application. Tiny solid particles will damage a column, and for this reason sample solutions should be passed through a fine filter directly before loading

Choice of column, solvent and flow rate

It is very difficult to draw a correlation between the behaviour of a mixture on tlc and the way it runs on hplc, and it is therefore preferable to carry out a few analytical hplc runs to find an appropriate solvent system and determine the quantity which can be separated. If you can use the identical type of column for your analytical work this is of course ideal. There are now sets of columns which run from micro analytical sizes through to large preparative scale, and have uniform characteristics through the series. We use 'Rainin *Dynamax'* columns which have a very sophisticated design and give excellent results for preparative work. The biggest factor which leads to loss of performance in hplc columns is the packing down of the solid phase which occurs with constant use and causes voids, particularly at the ends of the column. One of the features of Dynamax columns is that they are fitted with a compression joint, which closes the voids and enables the columns to perform well over extended periods of use. They can also be fitted with integral scrubber units which extend the life of the main column.

The sizes of the columns increase in regular steps and it is therefore very easy to correlate between the smaller 'analytical' columns and the larger 'preparative' columns. In fact the column which we use for analytical work is 4.5mm x 25cm, and would probably be viewed as a semi-prep column by an analytical chemist. However, it is very useful for method development, as it takes only a few minutes to equilibrate and to run. Indeed, it can be used as a small scale preparative column for quantities between about 5 and 40mg. For normal analytical hplc the intention is to develop a method which gives the best peak shape with good separation, and column overloading is therefore to be avoided. On the other hand, a good preparative method is one which will separate the components and allow you to 'get away' with maximum overloading, peak shape being largely irrelevant.

For full-scale preparative work either a 22.5mm or a 45mm column is normally used and it is easy to scale up to this size knowing the conditions used for the smaller column. If the columns are the same length the scale-up factor will depend on the area of the column surface, thus:-

$$\text{Scale-up factor, } F = \frac{\text{Area(large col)}}{\text{Area(small col)}} = \frac{\pi R^2 \text{(large)}}{\pi R^2 \text{(small)}} = \frac{(D/2)^2 \text{(large)}}{(D/2)^2 \text{(small)}}$$

Using these equation, the scale-up factor between the 4.5mm column and the 22.5mm column is 22.35. and between the 22.5mm and the 45mm it is 4. If the columns are not the same length then simply multiply the factor by the proportionate length difference (for example going from a 4.5mm x 12.25cm column to a 22.5 x 25cm column the scale-up factor would be 44.7). To work out the conditions for running the larger column simply multiply the flow rate and the quantity loaded on the small column by the scale-up factor and this should produce identical results on the large column. As a rough guide a 4.5mm x 25cm column runs at about 0.75ml/min and can be loaded with 5-35mg; a 22.5mm x 25cm column runs at about 16ml/min and can be loaded with 100-800mg and a 45mm x 25cm column runs at about 64ml/min and has a capacity of about 450mg to 3.2g. Once you have worked out a good system for prep hplc the run times are quite short, so that large amounts of material can be separated quite conveniently by multiple runs.

Solvents for hplc

All solvents used for hplc must be very high grade and must be degassed before use. Degassing can be achieved by bubbling helium through the solvent *via* a gas diffuser, by standing the bottle of solvent in an ultrasonic bath, or by stirring the solvent under vacuum. The solvent inlet line of the hplc system should always incorporate a filter to prevent small particles entering the system. Ethereal solvent mixtures are not very successful for hplc work and in general it is normally best to use a system where the more polar constituent is also the least volatile.

CHAPTER 10

Small Scale Reactions

10.1 Introduction

For the purposes of this chapter we will define small scale reactions as those involving reaction mixture volumes of less than 5ml. When performing organic reactions on this scale special problems arise, most notably:

1. Difficulties in measuring out small quantities of sensitive reagents.
2. Significant losses of material due to apparatus design.
3. Difficulties in excluding trace amounts of water from moisture-sensitive reactions.

Whenever reactions are performed, material losses are obtained as a consequence of the above problems. Normally these losses only account for a few percent of the total material, however this percentage can increase dramatically as the reaction scale decreases. For example if a moisture-sensitive reaction was carried out on a one mole scale, it would take 18g of water to completely stop the reaction occurring, however if the same reaction is carried out on a 0.1mmol scale, then only 1.8mg of water would completely quench the reaction.

The problem of weighing out small quantities of sensitive reagents is best solved by accurately weighing larger quantities, and making up solutions in an inert solvent, ideally the reaction solvent. Since the molarity of the solution is known, a quantitative aliquot of this solution can then be added to the reaction mixture using a syringe . This effectively reduces the problems of weighing out the material to those that exist in larger scale reactions, and discussed in earlier chapters. As a general rule many of the techniques used in setting up reactions discussed in the earlier chapters, can, with care, be applied to small scale reactions. Indeed there are a wide variety of miniature chemical apparatus commercially available for just this purpose.

This chapter will outline some of the more specialized techniques that can be employed to alleviate the problems associated with small scale, and that can be carried out without the requirement of relatively expensive specialized glassware.

10.2   Reactions at or below room temperature

When carrying out small-scale reactions at or below room temperature it is quite possible to use a conventional apparatus set-up. Most reactions are carried out in round-bottomed flasks, which are available in sizes down to 1ml. The main problems arise when you come to work up the reaction mixture. If an aqueous or organic extraction is required, then the material must be transferred to a separating funnel. This will inevitably lead to some loss of material during the transfer, but this should be minimal. The main problem arises from the fact that separating funnels rarely come in sizes below 10ml. In addition, because of their design there will always be some loss of material in the apparatus itself. This is mainly because the reaction mixture necessarily comes into contact with a large surface area of glassware, and retrieving material coated over this large area tends to be difficult. A useful alternative for extractions involving 2ml or less is to use a glass sample vial or small test-tube (Fig. 10.1). The reaction mixture can be washed into the sample vial, and the extraction solvent added. The lid of the vial is then put on, and the mixture shaken. Removal of the lid allows any pressure build-up to be released. Particular care should be taken when removing the lid to avoid spillage.

The required solvent layer is then removed using a Pasteur pipette. Three or four extractions are usually sufficient to recover the majority of the material. This technique is particularly straightforward for diethyl ether extractions of aqueous solutions in which the ether layer is required, since it can readily be pipetted from the top of the aqueous layer (Fig. 10.1). If you require the lower solvent layer, this can be recovered either by pipetting away the top layer, or by pipetting from the bottom of the vial. Because efficient separation of the two phases is required, it is preferable to use a

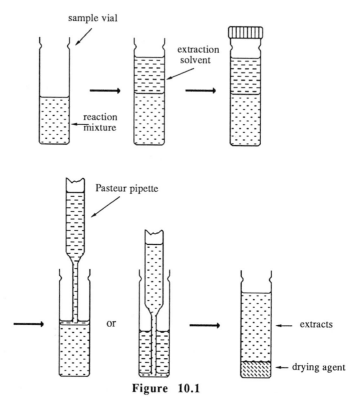

Figure 10.1

tall, thin vial rather than a short, fat one. A second vial containing drying agent can then be used to dry the extracts.

Removal of the drying agent is normally achieved by filtration of the solvent mixture, and on a small scale this is best achieved using a Pasteur pipette fitted with a cotton wool plug as the filtration apparatus (Fig. 10.2). Once the solvent has been transferred into the filtration pipette, it can be forced through the plug by applying pressure with a pipette teat. Evaporation of the solvent in the normal way then yields the crude reaction product. As stated earlier, material is inevitably lost with each transfer of apparatus. It is possible to cut down the number of transfers by using the sample vial as the reaction vessel. Very small magnetic fleas are now commonly available, and will fit most small sample vials. Consequently, with magnetic stirring, the vials can serve as small reaction vessels (Fig. 10.3). They are conveniently attached to the top of a magnetic stirrer machine using plasticine.

Figure 10.2

When capped, the vial is a sealed system, consequently this set-up is only useful for small scale reactions at room temperature that do not involve an increase or decrease in pressure inside the reaction vessel. For reactions at low temperature, or those requiring a positive pressure of an inert gas atmosphere, it is often more convenient to use a Pyrex test tube fitted with a septum (Fig. 10.3). In all other respects the arrangement is the same and, since Pyrex test tubes are available in a range of sizes, this apparatus can

Figure 10.3 Use of sample vial or test tube as a reaction vessel

cope with a range of reaction volumes down to about 0.2ml. Again the reaction vessel can also be used for a subsequent extraction procedure simply by replacing the septum with a bung.

10.3   Reactions above room temperature

Carrying out small scale reactions above room temperature, particularly those involving solvent at reflux, is very difficult. The problems are associated with preventing the evaporation of very small amounts of solvent, and material losses in the apparatus. This is usually caused by losses of material through ground-glass joint attachments of condensers to the reaction flask, and by inefficient condensation of the solvent vapour. One solution is to use a sealed tube (see Chapter 8) as the reaction vessel, and this is probably the equipment of choice for reactions involving volatile solvents ($\leq 50°C$) on scales below 1ml. For higher boiling solvents it is possible to use a one-piece apparatus, incorporating an air condenser system (Fig. 10.4). This apparatus can be conveniently constructed at the required size from a piece of Pyrex tubing. The air condenser is adequate enough to prevent the evaporation of higher boiling solvents ($\geq 100°C$). Alternatively, a one-piece apparatus incorporating a water condenser can also be used

Figure 10.4 Small scale air condenser and water condenser systems.

(Fig. 10.4). In this case the condenser system is more efficient, however construction of the apparatus is correspondingly more complex. In both cases the reflux apparatus can be easily constructed to allow reaction volumes down to about 0.5ml.

10.4 Reactions in nmr tubes

In many cases it is necessary to monitor closely the progress of a small scale reaction by methods other than tlc; one very useful alternative is nuclear magnetic resonance (nmr). With larger scale reactions this is simply done by removing an aliquot of the reaction mixture and recording its nmr spectrum. Obviously this approach cannot be applied to reactions involving relatively small quantities of material. The answer is to carry out the reaction in an nmr tube. Both 5mm and 10mm diameter nmr tubes can conveniently be used as reaction vessels (Fig. 10.5) in the same way as test-tubes were employed in Section 10.2.

Figure 10.5

The reaction can then be monitored by recording the spectrum of the reaction mixture directly. There are however several important points to note when using nmr tubes as reaction vessels:

1. The reaction solvent should be chosen carefully to ensure that it does not obscure the nmr region to be observed.
2. Magnetic stirring cannot be used because the magnetic flea in the nmr tube would interact with the nmr field causing severe broadening of the spectrum. Similarly the presence of paramagnetic material in the reaction mixture will lead to broadening of the spectrum.
3. For high-quality nmr spectra to be recorded, the reaction mixture should be homogeneous. The presence of solids in the reaction mixture will lead to poorly resolved spectra.

As a general rule you should use the reaction solvent that is normally employed for the type of reaction being carried out, however its deuterated equivalent must be used if ^{1}H nmr spectra are to be observed. Agitation of the reaction mixture is probably best achieved using sonication in an ultrasonic bath (Chapter 8), although periodic shaking will often suffice.

If you require to carry out the reaction at elevated temperatures then it is usually advisable to use a sealed nmr tube. Thick-walled nmr tubes are commercially available if the reaction mixture is required to withstand increased reaction pressures typical of those obtained in sealed tube experiments.

10.5 Purification of materials

The purification of small quantities of materials ($\leq$ 50mg) also poses certain problems. A number of simple techniques used are outlined below.

10.5.1 Distillation

By far the most convenient method of carrying out distillation on a small scale is to use a Kugelrohr apparatus (see Chapter 9). In order to cut down on losses through ground glass joint connections it is often necessary to use a one piece Kugelrohr bulb set (Fig. 10.6). This can be conveniently made to the size required from a piece of Pyrex tubing.

After distillation is complete the apparatus is left to cool, and the purified material recovered by cutting up the apparatus into three sections using a glass knife.

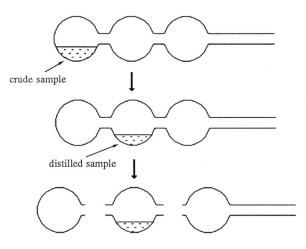

crude sample

distilled sample

Figure 10.6

10.5.2 Crystallization

Crystallizations on a small scale are most conveniently carried out using a Craig tube apparatus as described in Chapter 9.

10.5.3 Chromatography

All the normal chromatography techniques (see Chapter 9) can be used to purify small quantities of material. Indeed preparative hplc and glc are often more successful when small quantities of material are involved.

In the case of flash chromatography however, it is often impractical to simply scale down the equipment. A useful alternative is to employ a Pasteur pipette as the column. Such a column is easily constructed using a pipette containing a cotton wool plug (Fig. 10.7a). The pipette is then filled with the required adsorbent (typically silica gel). The amount of adsorbent used depends upon the quantity of crude sample to be purified, however it is inadvisable to fill the pipette more than three-quarters full, otherwise there is insufficient room for the solvent. Next, the eluting solvent is added to the top of the column and allowed to run through the column under gravity. More solvent is added to the top of the column as required. Once the solvent starts to appear at the bottom of the column, pressure can be applied using a pipette teat, forcing the solvent through at a faster rate. After about

Figure 10.7

two column-volumes of solvent have been passed through the silica it should be ready for use. The sample is applied to the top of the column in the usual way and pressure is applied using a pipette teat. The main difference between this arrangement and the more usual flash chromatography set-up is that the pressure applied to the top of the column is not constant. The teat is constantly being removed to allow the addition of more solvent to the top of the column. Consequently the solvent is not passing through the column at a constant rate. In most instances this does not appear to significantly affect the separations achieved. If, however, this proves to be a problem, a miniature chromatography column with solvent reservoir can easily be constructed from Pyrex glass tubing (Fig. 10.7b). With a cotton wool plug in the bottom this can be used in exactly the same way as the larger columns described in Chapter 9.

CHAPTER 11

Large Scale Reactions

11.1 Introduction

This chapter deals briefly with some of the specialized techniques required when working with larger scale reactions. For the purposes of this chapter we will define a large scale reaction as one involving reaction volumes of between 2 and 5 litres. Working on reaction volumes in excess of this usually requires the use of pilot-plant equipment and is beyond the scope of this book.

When working on larger reaction volumes, several problems arise as a consequence of the scale:

1. The use of syringes to add liquids to a reaction becomes impractical if you require to add volumes of more than 50ml.

2. Stirring the reaction mixtures can become a problem, because magnetic stirrers become ineffective for volumes much above 1 litre.

3. Control of the reaction temperature becomes more difficult as the reaction volume increases, because reaction mixtures will take much longer to heat up or cool down.

4. Exothermic reactions can prove to be a major problem on a large scale since they are prone to induction periods before reaction starts. After the induction period, the reaction can heat up rapidly and, unless extreme care is taken in these situations, the reaction can easily go out of control. It is recommended that very careful monitoring of the temperature is undertaken in such cases, and any addition of reagents which may lead to an exothermic reaction is carried out slowly.

5. Purification of materials on a large scale is often less easily carried out.

On the other hand, some problems that exist with smaller scale reactions can be less troublesome when working on large scale. For example, material losses that occur as a consequence of transferring the material between pieces of equipment become insignificant. Moisture-sensitive reactions are less of a problem because if traces of water get into the reaction they will only affect a very small percentage of the reaction mixture.

11.2   Carrying out the reaction

Figure 11.1

In most cases large versions of the standard laboratory equipment are adequate. Agitation is almost always achieved using a mechanical stirrer (see Chapter 8), since this is the only device powerful enough to stir large reaction volumes efficiently. As already mentioned, syringes tend to be useless for transferring large volumes of liquid and pressure-equalized dropping funnels serve well as their replacement. A typical set-up for a large scale reflux is outlined in Fig. 11.1. The pressure-equalized dropping funnel can be filled by removing the stopper and pouring in the required material or, if the material is moisture sensitive, then it can be transferred

Figure 11.2

into the dropping funnel *via* a cannula by replacing the stopper with a septum.

If the solution to be added from the dropping funnel requires cooling prior to addition it is possible to use a jacketed dropping funnel, with the cooling mixture (e.g. dry-ice/acetone) placed in the jacket. This is a common set-up encountered for low temperature reactions on larger scales (Fig. 11.2).

11.3 Purification of the products

Many purification techniques are not practical when dealing with large quantities of material. In general the most useful methods of purification that can be applied to large quantities of material are recrystallization for solids, and distillation or steam distillation for liquids. These techniques have already been discussed in previous chapters. Chromatography should be avoided if possible since it becomes a very expensive operation on large scale, but if it is necessary, then medium pressure liquid chromatography (mplc) as described in Chapter 9 is the method of choice.

CHAPTER 12

Characterization

12.1 Introduction

This chapter deals with the type of physical data that are required for the proper characterization of the purified product. No theory is discussed as this is well covered in other sources and, given good data, it is often possible to find a colleague (for example) who will help out if you are unable to interpret a spectrum. With inadequate data it will be difficult to be certain of the structure and purity of your product, and it will certainly be more difficult to interest the colleague referred to above!

It is important to acquire as much information as possible on your product. It might be 'obvious' from the nmr that the structure is what you think that it should be, but it is still necessary to record (at least) the ir and mass spectra. These might simply confirm the nmr data, or they might raise other structural possibilities.

The full set of routine physical data which could and, ideally, should be obtained on a pure compound is as follows; ir, uv, high field nmr (^{1}H and ^{13}C), and low and high resolution mass spectra, m.p. or b.p., microanalysis (for a new compound). If the compound is optically active then the optical rotation must be measured. Only mass spectroscopy and microanalysis from this list are destructive techniques, but modern techniques mean that only a small amount of material need be 'sacrificed'. Some general points concerning these techniques and the sample requirements are given below.

12.2   Nmr

Nowadays the ^{1}H nmr spectrum is often the first measurement taken. The size of sample required depends on the type of spectrometer used. A continuous wave machine operating at 90 MHz will need at least 10mg of a normal organic compound, probably more. Pulsed Fourier transform spectrometers require less, 5mg being a normal amount, and good spectra can be obtained using much smaller quantities. Most spectra are measured in deuteriochloroform ($CDCl_3$) although other solvents will be required from time to time. A typical solvent volume would be *ca.* 0.4-0.5ml in a 5mm tube. Routine measurement of the ^{13}C nmr spectrum usually requires more sample (25-50mg) but good spectra can be obtained on less, it simply takes more time.

The solution used must be free of paramagnetic metal ions (it usually is) and particles (it usually is not). Filtration through a small wad of cotton wool forced into a Pasteur pipette will usually remove sufficient particles to allow a good spectrum to be obtained.

The high field ^{1}H nmr spectrum will show up impurities containing protons. Given that the compound has been purified, the most common impurity peaks observed in the ^{1}H nmr spectrum are those from the last solvent used (for example, solvents used in crystallization or chromatography). This should be avoided, and it is always possible unless the boiling point of your product is close to the solvent (which it should not be) or your product is a crystalline solvate (not that common). Thorough exposure to high vacuum should suffice but some very viscous oils and gums will 'hold on' to solvent due to the very slow rate of diffusion. If warming in high vacuum fails to remove all solvent, and a 'clean' [1]H nmr spectrum cannot be obtained, then dissolve the sample in a small amount of $CDCl_3$ and evaporate. Repeat once or twice and most of the residual solvent should be $CDCl_3$ rather than (say) ethyl acetate. This will improve matters, but do not forget that your sample will still be impure on evaporation as it will contain residual $CDCl_3$.

12.3   Ir

The sample again needs to be free of impurities and solvents for infrared spectroscopy. There are various methods for sample preparation and which you choose will depend largely on the type of compound. The amount required is no more than a few milligrams. For a liquid sample the spectrum can be obtained using a thin film obtained by compressing a small drop between sodium chloride plates, or as a solution (usually in chloroform) using solution cells. The spectra of solids can be recorded either as mulls with a hydrocarbon ('Nujol', for example), or by mixing with KBr and compressing to form a thin disk. Which you use will depend upon the facilities available, and often on the usual working practice of your department.

12.4 Uv

Ultraviolet spectroscopy is only of use if your compound has a characteristic chromophore. There is little point trying to measure weak bands which will provide no information. However, it is of considerable value in several areas of research; for example, natural product isolation, heteroaromatic chemistry, porphyrin and related chemistry, and in the study of dyestuffs. The amount of material required is usually very small (fractions of a milligram) since the extinction coefficients are usually large. The sample must be as pure as possible and is dissolved in the solvent of choice (usually spectroscopically pure ethanol). The concentration must be known accurately before extinction coefficients can be calculated, and will vary depending upon the type of chromophore. An estimate of the concentration to use can be made if the extinction coefficients of compounds similar to that being studied are available. If this data is not available make up a solution accurately and dilute it (accurately!) until a reasonable spectrum is obtained.

12.5 Mass spectra

There are three pieces of useful information which can be obtained from mass spectroscopy; the molecular mass, composition, and the fragmentation pattern of your compound. The accurate molecular mass is of primary importance since this will confirm the composition of your compound. Fragmentation information might be of value for supporting the proposed structure, possibly by comparison with known compounds. The amount required is minimal (a few milligrams at most), and the material should be reasonably pure. If you are unable to obtain good microanalytical data the accurate mass measurement may provide an acceptable alternative.

12.6   M.p. and b.p.

These are usually straightforward. Always obtain a rough melting point before attempting to make accurate measurements and it is often useful to 'calibrate' the apparatus by measuring a known (pure!) compound with a similar m.p. to the product. If there is a significant discrepancy then a more reliable apparatus must be used. Do not forget to get the inaccurate apparatus repaired, and discard it if necessary The compound needs to be pure and free from dust, and the temperature must be raised very slowly as you near the melting point. If there is a range over which the compound melts (there usually is) then record it; do not estimate an 'average' reading. If a capillary tube is used, it is sometimes useful to examine the upper part of the tube for sublimate or distilled decomposition products.

If you have distilled your product to isolate and purify it then you should already have the information required for reporting the boiling point. It is important to quote the range of temperature (if observed) over which the compound distills, the pressure (measured as it is distilling), the vapour temperature (if measured), and the bath temperature. All these will be useful when you or anyone else come to repeat the work, and most of this information will be required at some time for a publication, report, or thesis.

12.7   Optical rotation

If your product is, or should be, optically active then the specific rotation will need to be measured and recorded. The precise value of this property is dependent on the wavelength of the light used, solvent, concentration, and temperature. Moreover, great care should be taken to exclude any by-products from the reaction since, although these might be present in small quantities, they might have very large rotations and make your measurements quite misleading. Clearly then, it is important to be sure of the purity of your product, and to make up the solution carefully and accurately. If you are unsure then make a measurement using a known compound before you try to measure the rotation of your product (assuming that the specific rotation of your product is not known). Usually you will use the sodium-D line and measure at ambient temperature, but be sure to record the concentration, solvent, wavelength, and temperature along with the actual value of the measured specific rotation. Occasionally optical rotatory dispersion and/or circular dichroism spectra will be required. These measurements will usually made by specialists and the specific requirements for your particular type of compound are best discussed with them.

12.8 Microanalysis

There are several schools of thought on this topic. Some maintain that all new compounds must be analysed, whereas others say that, with the modern array of physical methods (high resolution nmr spectroscopy and high resolution soft ionization mass spectroscopy, for example) the need for combustion analysis no longer exists. Many follow a middle course and use microanalysis for crystalline compounds which are available in sufficient quantity, and high resolution mass spectrometric measurements in all other cases. The course you take will depend upon circumstances (the requirements of your supervisor or the department, for example).

It goes without saying that the compound must be homogeneous and free from dust, inorganics, etc. For solids, careful recrystallization using pure, filtered solvents followed by equally careful filtration will usually suffice. For oils, distillation folllowed by sealing in an ampoule will provide acceptable samples. All the glassware involved must be clean and dry including the ampoule. Solids must be dried in high vacuum in a drying pistol to remove traces of solvent, and submitted in clean, dry vials. It is possible to obtain reasonable microanalytical data on oils which cannot be distilled by careful column chromatography using pure, distilled solvents followed by thorough pumping down in high vacuum.

12.9 Keeping the data

If you work for any length of time in the laboratory you will rapidly acquire a large number of spectra. It is important that you keep these safe and in proper order, with an unambiguous cross-referencing system so that you (and anyone else) can locate the spectra or measurements which apply to the product of a particular experiment (see Chapter 2 for detailed advice on this). Spectra are best kept in clearly labelled folders or binders of some description, preferably ones which allow for removable attachment of the spectra. The other data should be recorded in the laboratory notebook along with the experimental write up. If data sheets are used then all the data should be recorded on these as they are measured.

CHAPTER 13

The Chemical Literature

13.1 The structure of the chemical literature

13.1.1 Introduction

Consulting the literature is an essential element of chemical research. Whether you want to confirm the identity of your latest product, or check the feasibility of an exciting new idea, it would be both unscientific and counterproductive not to conduct a thorough literature search. Moreover, it is vital to the success of your work to keep abreast of developments in organic chemistry in general, and in your area in particular. The problem is that finding chemical information and keeping in touch with current developments are difficult and time consuming tasks.

We are the beneficiaries of almost one and a half centuries of research in organic chemistry. The accumulated output of that effort is an enormous body of data collected in a vast literature. It is estimated that over half a million articles (papers, patents, books, etc.) are published each year and the volume of publications will probably continue to rise. Searching such a huge body of work is a formidable problem but it must be emphasized that the time spent reading the literature is often more than repaid by the experimental time saved as a result.

This chapter is intended as a practical guide to efficient searching of the chemical literature; the main part is devoted to a description of the most important access routes to the primary literature, and a discussion of methods of tackling some common types of literature search. The chapter concludes with a section on methods of keeping in touch with the current literature. The reader is referred to two recent texts for more detailed information.[1,2]

13.1.2   The structure of the literature

Almost all chemical information is originally published in research journals, in patents, and in theses. These sources are called the primary literature and the goal of most literature searches is to find the original reports containing the required information. There are thousands of journals which publish papers on chemistry but in practice the great majority of papers which are of interest to the organic research chemist appear in just a hundred or so of these. This is still a dauntingly large body of information but there are several routes by which it can be searched and specific items of information located.

An important route, and one which is rapid and easy, is to tap the chemical knowledge of your colleagues and supervisors. Many of the people working around you are likely to be experts in their own fields. Another route is to use the secondary literature. This comprises review articles and books, in which the original literature has been organized and summarized, and reference books in which particular kinds of data have been collected together. Of course, finding the appropriate review or handbook is a problem in itself. A third route is *via* indexes which give the literature references for all of the information on a given compound, or procedure, or author etc. Prominent among these is Chemical Abstracts, which contains short summaries of just about every paper published on a chemical topic, as well as comprehensive indexes to these abstracts, and hence to the original papers. Finally there are computer databases, which offer unprecedented speed, reliability, and flexibility, but at a price!

13.2   Some important sources of chemical information

This section contains a description of structure, strengths, and weaknesses of four of the most important tools for locating information in the primary literature: Chemical Abstracts, Beilstein, the Science Citation Index, and computer databases. It is followed by a complementary section on how to carry out some specific kinds of searches.

1.   Y. Wolman, *Chemical Information, A Practical Guide to Utilization*, 2nd ed., Wiley, Chichester, 1988.
2.   R.E. Maizell, *How to Find Chemical Information*, 2nd ed., Wiley, Chichester, 1987.

13.2.1 Chemical Abstracts

Chemical Abstracts (CA) consists of two main parts, abstracts of every paper containing new chemical information, and indexes which provide access to the abstracts and thence to the original literature. It is published weekly and each issue contains a keyword index and an author index. The weekly issues are collected in volumes covering a six month period (one year, prior to 1962) and each volume contains author, chemical substance, formula, and general subject indexes. Every five years (ten years, prior to 1957) the indexes for the ten volumes are combined to give *Collective Indexes*. These indexes are the single most important and comprehensive information tool available to the chemist.

A search of Chemical Abstracts should begin with the appropriate index of the most recent volume and should progress backwards through the other volumes until the beginning of the period covered by the most recent Collective Index (currently the 11th - 1981-1986), at which stage the Collective Indexes are used to search the literature back to 1907. The most useful indexes are the chemical substance, formula, and general subject indexes and their use is described more fully in Section 13.3. Consulting the indexes will, in the first instance, lead to references to the abstracts, not directly to the literature. The references to the abstracts take the following form: **90**:*108753h* where **90** is the CA volume number and the abstract number is *108753*. Since 1967 abstracts have been numbered sequentially in each volume. Prior to that the references were of the form **46**:*13761a* where **46** is the volume number, *13761* is the column number, and the letter *a* indicates that the abstract is at the top of the column. Earlier still, a numerical superscript was used to indicate the position of the abstract in the column. The letters *R* or *P* before an abstract number indicate that the original work is a review or a patent, respectively.

The abstracts contain full bibliographic details of the original paper, and a summary of the principal new findings reported in the paper. A glance at the abstract will tell you if the original journal is likely to be accessible, what language the paper is in, and most importantly it will give an indication of whether the paper really does contain the information you require. Remember that many of the compounds described in the original paper will not be mentioned in the abstract but will be contained in the indexes. If the abstract looks promising all that remains is to locate the journal and consult the paper.

An *Index Guide* is published every eighteen months and contains invaluable information on the use of the indexes and the system of nomenclature used in CA. It is essential reading for serious users of Chemical Abstracts. Finally, the *Ring Systems Handbook* and its predecessors, the *Ring Index* and the *Parent Compound Handbook*, contain information on ring and cage systems and gives the names under which ring systems can be found in the Chemical Substance Index.

The great strengths of CA are that it provides comprehensive literature coverage, and it has extensive indexes. However, the coverage of the literature in the early years was not so rigorous, and Beilstein provides more thorough coverage of the pre-1949 literature.

13.2.2 Beilstein

Beilstein's Handbuch der Organischen Chemie, or Beilstein for short, is a huge (> 300 volumes) reference work which contains physical and chemical data for over one and a half million compounds. The compounds are organized according to a unique classification system and each volume contains a subject (actually compound) index and a formula index. Comprehensive literature coverage is attempted, so Beilstein contains essentially all the compounds of a given class, which were prepared from the beginning of organic chemistry to the date of publication of the most recent volume covering that class of compounds. A considerable amount of critically reviewed information, with references to the primary literature, is provided for each compound. This data includes the molecular structure, natural occurrence, methods of preparation, physical properties including references to papers containing spectral data, and chemical properties.

The Handbook consists of the original series of 27 volumes (the *Hauptwork, H*) and a number of supplementary series (*Ergansingbande, EI, EII,* etc.). Work on the supplements is constantly in progress. Coverage of the literature up to 1959 has almost been completed, and some progress has been made in bringing the coverage up to 1979. Cumulative indexes are only available for the pre-1930 literature. It is relatively easy to find data for any compound reported prior to 1930 by checking the cumulative formula index (Volume 29 in three subvolumes) which will give the volume and page numbers for the entries in H, EI and EII. Compounds of the same class will appear in the same volume of each series (although some of the volumes are now divided into several subvolumes). Thus if a compound is located using the cumulative index it is a simple matter to locate references in the later series, using the volume indexes for the same volume or using the *Beilstein System Number*. If a compound is not contained in the cumulative index it is best to try to identify which volume it should be contained in, using the classification system. A free booklet explaining how to use the Beilstein system is available from the publishers (Springer-Verlag).

Beilstein is the best and most comprehensive source of data for organic compounds prepared before 1930 and it is not particularly difficult to use. Its major weakness is the lack of data and cumulative indexes for more modern work.

13.2.3 Science Citation Index

Science Citation Index (SCI) is a combination of three indexes which provide coverage of all the important publications in the physical sciences. SCI is published every two months and is cumulated annually. There are cumulative indexes covering the period 1945-1979. It includes coverage of all of the major chemistry journals.

1. The *Source Index* lists the bibliographic details for the publications for each author/organization.

2. The *Permuterm Index* is based on combinations of keywords in the titles of the articles published in the journals which are covered by SCI. For example under the keyword 'epoxide' will be a list of other keywords, such as 'stereoselective', which occur in association with 'epoxide'. For each pairing there is a list of authors names, and looking these up in the *Source Index* will lead to the references for the original work.

3. The *Citation Index* is a unique feature which allows you to search the literature *forward* in time. The index entries are the names of the first authors of each paper which was cited in any paper published during the period covered by that issue. Its use is best illustrated with the aid of an example. Suppose that a researcher found a paper published in 1980, by S. Smith *et al.*, which contained some very interesting results, and he wanted to know if any further relevant work had

appeared. He would consult the annual indexes of the SCI from 1980 onwards. Each index contains an alphabetic list of *first* authors names and under S. Smith's name would be a chronological list of his/her publications. Under the entry for the paper of interest to our researcher there would be a list of papers, published during the period covered by that index, which cited it. It is reasonable to assume that any workers who followed up on the results in the Smith paper would have cited it in their own publications. Thus the list of papers which cited the original should include most of the work subsequently carried out in that area. Hence if you find an important paper you can use SCI to get a list of all the papers which subsequently referred to it. The drawback is that many of the references you find will not be relevant to your interest and there is no way of knowing which are relevant except by consulting the *Source Index*, which gives the titles of the papers, or by consulting the papers themselves.

The citation index is an extremely useful tool and we recommend that you carry out a search for every key paper you come across. You can also use it to find out who is referring to your own work.

13.2.4   Computer databases

The development of computer databases over the last decade has brought about a revolution in the way in which we search and store chemical information. The advantages of online searching include much greater speed, greater accuracy, and greater reliability. Some computer databases include material which cannot otherwise be searched directly, e.g. the full text of many major journals and reference books, and they generally contain more information than is accessible at the majority of institutional libraries. The principal advantage is much greater flexibility and power in carrying out searches. For example, it is possible to combine a number of searches in one using logical operators (oxidation AND (alcohol OR aldehyde)). Even more importantly it is possible to search for classes of compounds or compounds containing some specific substructure, searches which were almost impossible using printed indexes.

There are disadvantages too. Some databases do not include all of the material available in conventional form; for example, much of the early Chemical Abstracts is not available online. Another problem is that the software for online searching is relatively complex, so it is more difficult to learn and, as a result, online searches by inexperienced users can be unreliable. The increasing use of personal computers and graphical input and output have made database searching much easier but a good understanding of the software is still essential. Finally the cost of hardware, software, consumables, and the searches themselves, can be considerable.

The most important chemical databases include *CAS Online, CAS React, Beilstein, ORAC*, and *REACCS*. The online versions of CA and Beilstein are incomplete but the searching facilities are so powerful that they are indispensible. *CAS React, ORAC* and *REACCS* are databases of organic reactions which are extremely useful in searching for precedents for synthetic transformations. Many other databases are available so you should ask at your library for a list of those accessible to you. It is not possible to describe the operation of the databases here but you should get some help from your librarians or your supervisor and learn how these very powerful tools can help you.

13.3   How to find chemical information

13.3.1 How to do searches

The following are some basic rules for guidance in searching the literature.
1. Clearly define the goals of your search.
2. Discuss the problem with your colleagues and supervisors; they may have some valuable expertise.
3. Decide which information sources to use.
4. Start with the current literature and work backwards, the recent literature will contain references to earlier work.
5. When you find a key paper, check it carefully for references to relevant earlier work, and also work forward in time by carrying out a Science Citation Index search.
6. Keep a complete record of your search, noting all the sources you used and the information you obtained (e.g. lists of CA abstract numbers and their contents). This is invaluable if you have to carry out related searches later. It is advisable to keep a separate notebook for recording your literature searches, the information you accumulate will build into a very useful resource.

13.3.2   How to find information on specific compounds

The chief sources of data for particular compounds are Chemical Abstracts and the numerous reference handbooks, including Beilstein. Information on relatively simple compounds can often be obtained from handbooks such as the following:

1. The catalogues of major chemicals suppliers.
2. *CRC Handbook of Chemistry and Physics*, R.C. Weast Ed., CRC Press.
    CRC Handbook for Organic Compound Identification.
    CRC Handbook of Data on Organic Compounds.
    These sources contain physical and chemical data for a large number of organic compounds.
3. *The Dictionary of Organic Compounds,* 5th ed. Chapman and Hall.
    The Dictionary of Organometallic Compounds.
    These multivolumed works quote physical properties and references to the preparation and properties of about 75,000 compounds and many derivatives. Both have name and formula indexes, kept up to date by the publication of annual supplements. They are available online.
4. Several extensive collections of spectral data are available. The most extensive of these are produced by Sadtler Research Laboratories and cover ir, Raman, uv, ^{1}H nmr, ^{13}C nmr, and mass spectra. The Aldrich Chemical Company has produced three excellent collections of data: ir, FT-ir, and ^{1}H nmr.

For data on more complex structures it is usually necessary to turn to Beilstein or CA. Beilstein is in fact a giant handbook containing data for *all* organic compounds published in the timespan of the volumes which are available. Its use is described in Section 13.2.2. The best way to find specific compounds in Chemical Abstracts is to start with the *Formula Index*. The formulas are listed in order of increasing number of carbons, then increasing number of hydrogens, and then increasing numbers of the other elements in alphabetical order. Under each formula is a list of names, and for each substance there is a list of abstract numbers. It is best to scan through the list of names to try to identify the compound you want and then, armed with the correct CA name, use the *Chemical Substance Index*. The *Chemical Substance Index* has the advantage that, for each substance, it gives a list of keywords (isolation, preparation, etc.) followed by the abstract numbers. The keyword list makes it much easier to identify which abstracts are most likely to contain the information you require. With a little experience you may prefer to use the *Chemical Substance Index* directly but the complexities of nomenclature and indexing preclude any further discussion here. Note that prior to the 9th Collective Index, the *Chemical Substance* and *General Subject Indexes* were combined in the *Subject Index*.

13.3.3   How to find information on classes of compounds

Finding information about a broader area, such as a class of compounds is usually more difficult than finding data about a specific compound. It is usually best to begin by consulting books on the area, and then progress to more specialized monographs and reviews, before consulting the primary literature.

Good starting places include *Comprehensive Organic Chemistry, Comprehensive Organometallic Chemistry* and *Comprehensive Heterocyclic Chemistry* (Pergamon Press), which are multivolume texts giving a detailed overviews of the title areas. A much more detailed treatment of many common classes of compounds is contained in the series *The Chemistry of the Functional Groups* edited by S. Patai (Wiley). This excellent series consists of over 30 volumes (in nearly 60 parts) each of which contains reviews on all aspects of the chemistry of one particular functional group. Other multivolume series include *The Chemistry of Heterocyclic Compounds - A Series of Monographs* (Wiley) and *Rodd's Chemistry of Carbon Compounds* (Elsevier). In addition there are many review series devoted to the chemistry of particular classes of compounds, including the *Specialist Periodical Reports* published by the Royal Society of Chemistry. See Section 13.3.4 for a list of sources of information on synthetic methods for families of compounds.

Finding individual books or reviews is more difficult. A good starting point is your library, glance along the shelves and consult the catalogue. A more systematic method is to use *Index of Reviews in Organic Chemistry* (Royal Society of Chemistry) or *Index to Scientific Reviews* (Institute for Scientific Information) to locate books and reviews.

Manual searching of *Chemical Abstracts* is not a good method for tackling this kind of search because the indexing policy means that very few articles will be cited under a general heading such as aldehydes. *CAS Online* will usually give much better results because a wider range of subject terms can be used in the search. If you are looking for information on a highly specific structure type, a substructure search of *CAS Online* should give essentially 100% recovery of the relevant references.

13.3.4   How to find information on synthetic methods

The reference books on the chemistry of classes of compounds which are listed in Section 13.3.3 are good starting points in this case too. Additionally there are several major works devoted specifically to synthetic methods. *Comprehensive Organic Synthesis* (Pergamon), a nine volume overview of the area, is due to be published in 1989. Other useful texts include *Compendium of Organic Synthetic Methods* (Wiley) and *Survey of Organic Synthesis* (C.A. Buehler and D.E. Pearson, Wiley), and no list would be complete without the excellent *Advanced Organic Chemistry, Reactions, Mechanisms, and Structures* by J. March (Wiley). *Organic Syntheses* (Wiley) is a compilation of carefully checked procedures with full experimental details and is an excellent source of representative synthetic procedures. Numerous syntheses of natural products are reviewed in the volumes of *The Total Synthesis of Natural Products* edited by Ap Simon (Wiley). *Organic Reactions* (Wiley) is an ongoing series containing reviews of specific reactions. A relatively new series called *Best Synthetic Methods* (Academic Press) aims to present critical reviews of the preferred methods for carrying out common transformations. *Reagents for Organic Synthesis* (L.F. Fieser and M. Fieser, Wiley) is the best source of information on the preparation, purification, and use, of reagents, whereas *Synthetic Reagents* (S.S. Pizey, Wiley) provides detailed reviews of a smaller number of particularly common reagents.

Two excellent series provide annual coverage of developments in synthetic chemistry. Theilheimer's *Synthetic Methods of Organic Chemistry* provides thorough coverage of the synthetic literature and is organized according to a unique (and easily learned) system of classifying the transformations taking place. Theilheimer is available online *via* the *Chemical Reactions Documentation Service* (Derwent Publications Ltd.) and *REACCS* (Molecular Design Ltd.). *Annual Reports in Organic*

Synthesis (Academic Press) is a well organized collection of representative synthetic transformations and it is up to date and very easy to use.

Chemical Abstracts is not particularly useful for the same reasons as outlined in Section 13.3.3. Again *CAS Online* is much better but the best online sources are the databases of synthetic methods. Databases such as *ORAC*, *SYNLIB* and *REACCS* contain tens of thousands of transformations, chosen for their synthetic value. They can be searched very easily using graphical input and output, and powerful software features allow you to perform highly specific searches which cannot be carried out in any other way.

13.4 Current awareness

Keeping in touch with the current literature is a difficult and time consuming exercise but it is vital to your development as a chemist, and to the success of your research. You should aim to read through at least 6-12 of the most important journals in your field and the best way of doing this is to set aside a specific period each week for reading the periodicals. You should also scan the review journals (*Angewandte Chemie,International Edition in English, Chemical Society Reviews, Chemical Reviews, Synthesis,* and *Tetrahedron*) and magazines such as *Chemical and Engineering News, Chemistry and Industry* and *Chemistry in Britain*.

As if this is not enough, there is still the problem of how to cover the hundreds of other chemistry periodicals. The only practical method of doing this is to use compilations of abstracts. You could read Chemical Abstracts itself but this is too large and a much better choice is one or more of the titles in the *CA Selects* series, which only contain abstracts relating to a particular area. However, wider literature coverage is essential and a good approach is to read one of the periodicals which abstracts new compounds and reactions. *Methods of Organic Synthesis* (Royal Society of Chemistry) and the more comprehensive *Index Chemicus* (Institute of Scientific Information) are good examples of this genre.

All of this effort will be wasted if you do not keep good records of what you have read. Building your own computer database is an increasingly practical way of doing this but for now the simplest method is to use a card file. Make a record of each important paper on an index card.

Include the bibliographic details and an abstract of the key results in the paper. The pile of cards is not of much use unless it is properly filed. Many filing systems, each with its own strengths and weaknesses, can be conceived but one possibility deserves special mention, at least as a starting point. *Annual Reports in Organic Synthesis* (Section 13.3.4) is essentially a compilation of index cards in book form, and the systematic way in which the material is organized could serve as a useful model for your system. As time progresses you can modify this system to adapt it to your own interests and requirements.

CHAPTER 14

Special Procedures

14.1 Introduction

This section deals with some of the specialized procedures which might be encountered. All the topics covered here have one thing in common, namely that the particular type of apparatus used will vary from one laboratory to another and accordingly detailed instructions will not be given here for any one piece of apparatus. Representative systems are shown, and common operating procedures discussed. Often there will be someone in the department who is responsible for, or has particular expertise in, one of these techniques. If this is the case then always consult this person before you intend attempting the reaction.

14.2 Catalytic hydrogenation

Caution: Extreme care must be taken whenever hydrogen gas and active catalysts are used. Observe local safety precautions strictly.

If you are unfamiliar with catalytic hydrogenation or with the particular local apparatus, do find someone with experience of the apparatus and technique, and familiarize yourself with the manipulations and precautions *before* attempting the reaction.

The reduction of organic compounds using hydrogen and a catalyst is a reaction which is often encountered. Most catalytic hydrogenations are carried out at atmospheric pressure, and organic chemistry laboratories will have their own 'atmospheric' hydrogenation apparatus. These consist of a gas burette (or burettes) connected to a hydrogen supply, and to the reaction flask (see Section 6.3 for details of gas burettes). A typical arrangement is shown in Fig. 14.1 and the operation is simple in principle. A volume of hydrogen (more than the theoretical amount whenever possible) is transferred to the burette, with the reaction vessel containing the solvent, catalyst, and reactant, and the initial volume noted. The reaction is then agitated (stirred or shaken) and the uptake of hydrogen monitored using the burette. The detailed operation will depend upon the precise equipment which is used, but a written step-by-step procedure should be available. It is important to follow the procedure closely, and to consider the effect of opening any tap *before* doing so.

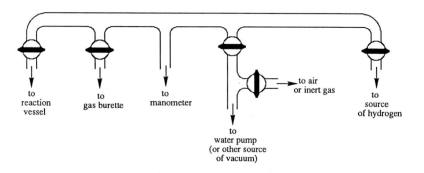

Figure 14.1 Schematic diagram of an atmospheric hydrogenator

When filling the reaction flask, add the catalyst first, followed by the solvent, and then your substrate. Addition of an active batch of catalyst to solvent can cause fires. Do make sure that all air is removed from the system by following the detailed procedure which applies to your particular system, and when the reaction is over, ensure that as much residual hydrogen is removed as possible; again, follow the procedure. Ensure that a safety screen is used as much as possible throughout the whole operation.

Filtration of the reaction mixture *must* be done carefully. Filter through a pad of Celite on a sintered glass funnel, but do not allow the catalyst to dry out. Wash through with more solvent and dispose of the wet catalyst/Celite mixture properly. Most laboratories have a special bottle for catalyst residues; use it. Numerous fires have resulted from wet catalyst residues being placed in a waste bin, since the residue dries out in the air and ignites. Do not attempt a catalytic hydrogenation until you know what to do with the catalyst residue.

The above procedure is sometimes inconvenient for small scale work (it depends upon the type of hydrogenation system available), and we often resort to the use of a small balloon of hydrogen connected to the reaction *via* a three-way tap, which is also connected to a manifold. This technique is illustrated in Fig. 14.2.

Fill the balloon with hydrogen (several times to remove air) and connect it to the flask. Connect the three-way tap to the manifold, open to vacuum (carefully) and then to the inert gas (Fig. 14.2a). Several cycles will be required. Then turn the tap so as to isolate the system from the manifold, and allow hydrogen to enter the flask (Fig. 14.2b). The reaction can then be monitored in the usual way. When the reaction is over, vent the excess hydrogen from the balloon (*safely*) to a fume cupboard (Fig. 14.2c). Residual hydrogen can be removed from the system by the use of several cycles of evacuation followed by admission of inert gas using the manifold as above (Fig. 14.2a). *All precautions referred to in the use of the atmospheric hydrogenator must be observed here of course.*

(a)   (b)   (c)

Figure 14.2   Small scale hydrogenation using a balloon

Medium- and high-pressure hydrogenations require specialized equipment and great care. This equipment usually consists of a metal reaction vessel and the appropriate 'plumbing' to allow its safe pressurization with hydrogen. These reactions are potentially most hazardous, and *must* be carried out under the close supervision of the person who is responsible for the apparatus.

14.3   Photolysis

Caution: Ultraviolet radiation is very damaging to the eyes and skin.

The reactor must be properly screened. Wear special protective goggles, or better still a face shield which offers protection against ultraviolet radiation if the apparatus is to be adjusted (or samples taken) while the lamp is on. When doing this also protect the hands with gloves and make sure that no other areas of skin would be exposed to radiation in the event of an accident. It is much safer to turn off the lamp when such manipulations are being carried out.

Preparative photochemical reactions are usually carried out in an immersion-well reactor, the usual design is shown in Fig. 14.3.

Figure 14.3   Photochemical reactor

Air is removed from the solvent by bubbling nitrogen or argon up through the solution *via* the sintered glass disk. Ensure that the correct choice of lamp has been made. Low pressure lamps emit most of their radiation at 254nm, are low power (up to ~ 20W) and require a quartz immersion well (not Pyrex). Most preparative reactions use the much higher power (100-400W) medium pressure lamps, as these emit their radiation over a much wider range (mainly at ~ 365nm with other bands at both shorter and longer wavelength). Occasionally a filter will be required and it is important that the correct one is used (this will be specified in the preparation being followed).

Reactions are usually run at fairly high dilution (up to ~ 0.05M) and the solvent should be pure and chosen with care. It must not decompose under ultraviolet irradiation and should not absorb at the wavelength being used for the reaction. Work up often involves no more than evaporation of the solvent followed by purification.

14.4   Ozonolysis

Caution: Ozone is toxic, and ozonides potentially explosive.

Ozone is generated using a commercial ozonator (or ozonizer) which can produce a concentration of up to 8% in oxygen, and which will be available in most organic research establishments. The operation of these is very simple providing that the instructions for the particular device are followed carefully. Make sure that these are consulted before attempting the reaction.

The compound to be ozonized is dissolved in the appropriate solvent, and cooled to the desired temperature. Ozone is then passed through the solution until no more starting material remains. For most purposes an excess of ozone can be used. It can be difficult to avoid this, but an indicator which can be added to the solution to show you when there is free ozone in the solution can sometimes be most valuable in avoiding over-oxidation.[1]

The work up depends upon the desired product, but will include a reagent which reacts with the ozonide. This reagent is almost always added in excess, and before any product isolation is attempted. Make sure that you allow plenty of time for the ozonide to react, as isolation of ozonides is to be avoided due to their potential for violent explosive decomposition. Once the ozonide is fully reacted the reaction can be processed in the usual manner.

1.   T. Veysoglu, L.A. Mitscher, and J.K. Swayze, *Synthesis*, 1980, 807.

14.5   Flash   vacuum   pyrolysis   (fvp)

This technique is not often encountered in synthetic organic chemistry, but it can prove invaluable in some circumstances. As with most of the topics in this chapter, the exact type of apparatus used will depend on what is available in your department. One simple (schematic) set up is shown in

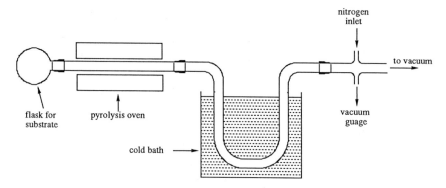

Figure 14.4   Schematic representation of an apparatus for FVP

Fig. 14.4. It is important to vaporize the substrate at the appropriate rate, and to make sure that the thermolysis temperature is correct. If this information is not available then some experimentation will inevitably have to be carried out. A typical vaporization rate might be between 0.5 and 1.0g per h.

As with all high vacuum work, care must be taken. After all of the substrate has passed through the hot tube, turn off the furnace and allow to cool to room temperature (still under vacuum). Then turn off the pump and admit nitrogen to atmospheric pressure. Remove the traps to a fume cupboard and allow to warm to room temperature, and work up in the usual way. If the desired product is unstable towards air, water, or is simply very reactive, then a more sophisticated pyrolysis system might be required, and more elaborate work up procedures used.

14.6   Liquid   ammonia   reactions

Caution: Ammonia is a powerful irritant, toxic, and the gas is flammable.   Conduct all reactions in an efficient fume cupboard and avoid all contact with the liquid.

Liquid ammonia (b.p. -33ºC) is a solvent which is not encountered frequently, but which does have several important general uses, in particular 'dissolving metal' reductions ('Birch' type reductions) and most reactions involving lithium amide or sodium amide as bases. Ammonia gas from a cylinder is condensed directly into the flask (Fig. 14.5).

Figure 14.5

The apparatus is set up as in Fig. 14.5 and a rapid flow of ammonia is used to flush out the system. A small volume of acetone (or ethanol) is poured into the condenser, and solid carbon dioxide pellets are added (*very slowly at first*) until the condenser is nearly full. The ammonia will begin to condense, and when the required volume is obtained, the ammonia flow is shut off and the gas inlet replaced by a septum or stopper. If undried impure ammonia will suffice, and often it will, then the reaction is carried out as normal. A cooling bath can be added if a long reaction time is anticipated, or if a temperature below -33ºC is required (see Chapter 8).

If dry liquid ammonia is needed this is usually obtained by distillation off sodium. The appropriate volume of ammonia is condensed as above and small pieces of sodium are added to produce a blue solution. The ammonia can then be distilled using a normal distillation apparatus (Chapter 9) except that the receiver (usually the reaction flask) is cooled in a solid carbon dioxide/acetone cooling bath. The ammonia in the distillation flask must remain blue throughout). The distillation apparatus is disconnected from the receiver which is then fitted with a cold-finger condenser and the reaction carried out as normal. The work up is usually simple. Solid ammonium chloride is added *carefully* and the ammonia allowed to evaporate (Chapter 9). The product may then be isolated and purified in the usual way.

CHAPTER **15**

'Trouble Shooting': What to do when things do not work

Do not despair - yet...

Some reactions will not work, for proper chemical reasons associated with the substrate. These may or may not be 'obvious' (many things become 'obvious' with hindsight). Do not jump to the conclusion that you have encountered such a reaction. Before you can conclude that this is the case a number of possibilities must be explored.

The first and most obvious is to make sure that the starting material is pure, dry, and free from solvents, and that it is indeed what you think it is. A critical perusal of *all* the analytical and spectroscopic data will usually be sufficient. If you have used several batches of starting material then do make certain that the spectra which you check are from the batch which you used in the failed reaction. If necessary, re-run the spectra to ensure that the starting material has not partially decomposed, or picked up moisture.

Once you are certain that the problem does not lie with the starting material, check the solvent. Many reactions will not work if the solvent is not anhydrous; methods for obtaining anhydrous solvents are given in Chapter 4. Tetrahydrofuran (THF) is very commonly used, and is usually dried by distillation off sodium/benzophenone; however it is possible collect *wet* THF from a bright blue distillation pot (which means that the solvent is dry in this part of the still). This problem is encountered when a still head is used to collect the solvent, but insufficient time has been allowed at reflux before collection is commenced. One way to check this is to repeat the reaction, but take a sample of the THF used (before introducing it into the reaction flask) and add a little sodium hydride (dispersion in oil) (*care*). If immediate hydrogen evolution is observed, the solvent is wet. The remedy is to allow more time at reflux before collecting the solvent, if this does not work the drying agents might need recharging.

Another source of water could be the inert gas which you are using; make sure that the drying agent (if used) used is still working renew it if necessary. Failing this, try the reaction under argon, which usually contains much less moisture than nitrogen. Check the manifold and renew any suspect tubing.

With pure starting materials, and anhydrous solvent and atmosphere, the reagent(s) must be suspected. If it is possible to purify them, do so, and make sure that you are handling them correctly (see Chapter 5). It will not be practical to purify some reagents, for example alkyllithiums, and in this case the quality should be checked by titration where possible. It is unwise to purchase a reagent (from any source) and to take for granted the quoted molarity and purity; even the most reputable suppliers are fallible and occasionally make mistakes.

If starting material, reagents, solvent, and inert gas are all as they should be then it might be you! You might be inadvertently carrying out the reaction in such a way that it will not work. For example, is the temperature correct, is the *concentration* of reactant and reagent correct, is too much or too little time being allowed at a particular stage? There are many possibilities. To test this it is advisable to carry out the same reaction but use a substrate which is known from the literature to react properly. If this is successful, and your desired reaction is not then you have found a reaction which does not work on your substrate, and alternative conditions (different metal ions, different Lewis acid etc.) might be required. Above all, if the reaction is an important one, do not give up; perhaps you could take the opportunity to develop a new reagent or procedure which will work!

CHAPTER 16

Example Reactions

16.1 Preparation of n-butyllithium[1]

A dry, 250ml, round-bottomed flask fitted with Liebig condenser and a septum is flushed with dry argon and the reaction vessel placed under a positive pressure of argon (Fig. 16.1). Freshly cut lithium wire (5g, 0.71mol) is placed in the reaction flask, and dry hexanes (80ml) added to the reaction flask *via* syringe. The reaction mixture is sonicated using an ultrasonic bath. n-Butyl chloride (37ml, 0.35mol) in dry hexanes (50ml) is added dropwise to the lithium suspension *via* syringe over a period of about 10min. Reaction begins after a short induction period (ca. 5-10min) causing the reaction mixture to warm and producing a purple precipitate. The reaction mixture is sonicated for a further 3h, and then filtered under an argon atmosphere (see Chapter 9). The resulting n-butyllithium solution is collected in a 250ml conical flask which is subsequently fitted with a septum. The conical flask is flushed with argon such that the n-butyllithium solution remains under an inert atmosphere. As long as the solution is protected from atmospheric moisture and oxygen, it can be stored in the conical flask until required for use. The molarity of the n-butyllithium solution produced should be about 1.8M, and this can be checked by titration (see Section 16.2).

1.   H. Gilman, J.A. Beel, C.G. Brannen, M.W. Bullock, G.E. Dunn, and L.S. Miller, *J. Am. Chem. Soc.*, 1949, **71**, 1499.

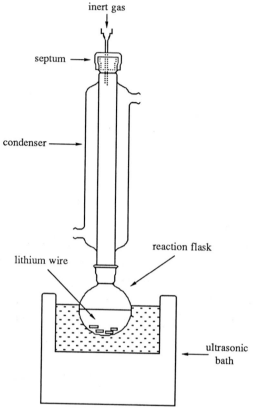

Figure 16.1

16.2   Titration of n-butyllithium

Red-orange

A dry, 2ml, round-bottomed flask or small Pyrex test tube fitted with a
magnetic stirrer bar and septum is flushed with argon, and then placed under
a positive pressure of argon (Fig. 16.2).

inert gas

septum →

reaction mixture →

Figure 16.2

1,3-Diphenyl-2-propanone p-toluenesulphonylhydrazone (113 mg, 0.5mmol)[2] is placed in the flask, and dry tetrahydrofuran (2ml) added *via* syringe. The reaction mixture is stirred rapidly to dissolve the hydrazone, and the n-butyllithium solution is added dropwise to the colourless solution until the orange-red end-point is observed. At this point the volume of n-butyllithium solution added is noted, and from this the molarity of the solution is calculated using the following equation:

Molarity of n-butyl lithium solution = Volume of solution used × 1000

In order to obtain an accurate titre it is necessary to carry out this titration at least three times and calculate the average of the results obtained.

16.3   Aldol reaction: preparation of 5-hydroxy-2,2-dimethyl-5-phenylpentan-3-one[3]

$$\xrightarrow[\text{2) Benzaldehyde}]{\text{1) LDA}}$$

A dry, 100ml, round-bottomed flask fitted with septum and magnetic stirrer

2.   For a discussion of the varoious titration methods see, J. Suffert, *J. Org. Chem.*, 1989, **54**, 509.
3.   H.O. House, D.S. Crumrine, A.Y. Teranishi, and H.D. Olmstead, *J. Am. Chem. Soc.*, 1973, **95**, 3310.

Figure 16.3

bar is flushed with argon, then placed under a positive pressure of argon. Anhydrous diisopropylamine (2.9ml, 20.8mmol) is added to the flask *via* syringe, followed by dry diethyl ether (20ml). The reaction mixture is cooled to -78°C using a dry ice-acetone cooling bath (Fig. 16.3). n-butyllithium (11.6ml of a 1.8M solution in hexanes, 20.8mmol) added dropwise *via* syringe to the stirred mixture. After addition of the n-butyl-lithium is complete the reaction mixture is stirred for 10min at -78°C allowing complete formation of lithium diisopropylamide then a solution of 3,3-dimethylbutan-2-one (2.4ml, 19.2mmol) in dry diethyl ether (5ml) is added dropwise via syringe to the reaction mixture. After stirring at -78°C for 10min, benzaldehyde (2.4g, 19.2mmol) is added and the mixture stirred for a further 30min. The reaction is quenched by careful addition of 1M hydrochloric acid (50ml), and the resulting mixture allowed to warm to room temperature before being transferred to a 250ml separating funnel. The mixture is extracted with diethyl ether (3x50ml) and the combined etheral extracts washed with saturated aqueous sodium chloride solution (50ml). The organic extracts are then dried over magnesium sulphate, and the solvent removed on a rotary evaporator to give the crude product as an oil. Kugelrohr distillation gives 5-hydroxy-2,2-dimethyl-5-phenylpentan-3-

one (3.2g, 80%) as a colourless oil (b.p. 86°C/0.07mmHg) which solidifies on standing to give a colourless solid m.p. 22-23°C.

16.4 Preparation of ethyl(triphenylphosphoranylidene) acetate[4]

A 2 litre, 3-necked, round-bottomed flask, fitted with thermometer, mechanical stirrer, and dropping funnel (Fig. 16.4) is charged with triphenylphosphine (104.8g, 0.4mol) and toluene (250ml). The solution is stirred vigorously while ethyl bromoacetate (74.4g, 0.4mol) is added dropwise at a rate that maintains the reaction temperature at, or slightly above, room temperature. After the addition is complete, the reaction mixture

Figure 16.4

4.   R.W. Lang and H.-J. Hansen, *Org. Synth.*, 1984, **62**, 202.

is stirred at room temperature for 2h, then the colourless phosphonium salt precipitate is filtered off, and washed first with cold toluene (250ml) and then petroleum ether (150ml). The crude phosphonium salt is dissolved in water (2 litres), placed in a separatory funnel, and further organic impurities removed by washing with diethyl ether (2x400ml). The aqueous solution is transferred to a 5 litre beaker, and 2% alcoholic phenolphthalein (10 drops) added. The solution is cooled in an ice-water bath and stirred vigorously by means of a glass rod as 2N aqueous sodium hydroxide is added slowly until the pink end-point is reached. At this stage as much water as possible is decanted from the precipitated phosphorane, then ethyl acetate (1.5 litres) is added. The resulting two phase mixture is transferred to a separating funnel and the aqueous layer removed. The ethyl acetate solution is dried over magnesium sulphate and evaporated on a rotary evaporator, to give ethyl (triphenylphosphoranylidene)acetate (122g, 88%) as a cream solid, m.p. 124-126°C.

16.5   Claisen rearrangement[5]

A mixture of cinnamyl alcohol (3.3g, 25mmol), triethyl orthoacetate (4.6ml, 25mmol) and hexanoic acid (2 drops) is placed in a 50ml, 2-necked, round-bottomed flask equipped with a thermometer, Dean-Stark trap, and condenser (Fig. 16.5). The solution is heated in an oil bath, allowing the ethanol produced to distil out of the reaction mixture and collect in the trap. After 2h, the distillation of ethanol slows, and more hexanoic acid (1 drop) is added. Additional portions of hexanoic acid are added after 3 and 4h. After 4.5h, at least 2ml of ethanol should have been collected, and tlc (25% diethyl ether - 75% petroleum ether) should indicate complete consumption of the cinnamyl alcohol. Over the 4.5h period the internal temperature rises from 100°C to 166°C. The solution is then allowed to cool and a solution of potassium hydroxide (2g, 35mmol) in water (3ml) and methanol (8ml) is added. The Dean-Stark trap is replaced by a condenser and then the mixture

5.   F. B. Gonzalez and P. A. Bartlett., *Org. Synth.*, 1985, **64**, 175.

Figure 16.5

is heated under reflux for 45min under nitrogen (Fig. 16.6). After the
alkaline solution has cooled to room temperature, water (30ml) is added, the
mixture washed with diethyl ether (20ml) and then acidified with
concentrated hydrochloric acid. The acidic aqueous solution is extracted
with diethyl ether (3x20ml), and the extracts dried over magnesium
sulphate. Filtration and removal of the solvent on a rotary evaporator then
gives the crude product. Flash chromatography on silica gel (20% diethyl
ether - 80% petroleum ether) gives the purified 3-phenyl-4-pentenoic acid as
a pale yellow solid which can be recrystallized from petroleum ether (m.p.
44-46°C).

nitrogen

condenser

thermometer

oil bath

stirrer-hotplate

Figure 16.6

16.6 Hydrogenation of maleic acid[6]

$$\text{maleic acid} \quad \xrightarrow[\text{PtO}_2]{\text{H}_2 \text{ , Ethanol}} \quad \text{succinic acid}$$

A 50ml, round-bottomed flask fitted with a magnetic stirrer bar is charged with maleic anhydride (2.32g, 20mmol) platinum oxide (20mg), and ethanol (30ml). The flask is fitted with a 3-way tap connected to a vacuum line, and balloon filled with hydrogen (Fig. 16.7). The reaction flask is sequentially evacuated and purged with hydrogen three times, and then left under a slight

6.   R. Adams and V. Voorhees, *Org. Synth. Col.*, 1932, **1**, 61.

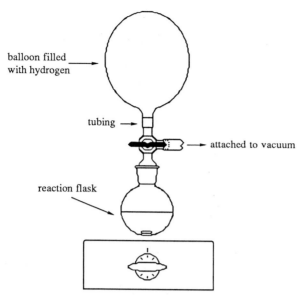

balloon filled
with hydrogen

tubing

attached to vacuum

reaction flask

Figure 16.7

positive pressure of hydrogen maintained by the balloon.

The reaction mixture is stirred at room temperature for 1h, the hydrogen balloon removed, and the mixture filtered through a pad of silica gel (3g) to remove the catalyst. The solvent is the removed on a rotary evaporator to give a white solid which can be crystallized from about 2ml of boiling water, to give succinic acid (2g, 84%), m.p. 187-189°C.

CHAPTER 17

Safety

17.1 Safety is your primary responsibility

Chemical laboratories are potentially dangerous workplaces and accidents in the lab can have serious and tragic consequences. However, if you are aware of potential hazards, and work with due care and attention to safety, the risk of accidents is small. Some general guidelines for safety in the laboratory are presented in this section. In addition to these principles you *must* be familiar with the safety regulations in force in your area and the rules and guidelines applied by the administrators of your laboratory.

Your supervisor has a responsibility to warn you of the dangers associated with your work, and you should always consult him/her, or a safety officer, if you are unsure about potential hazards. However, your own safety, and that of your colleagues in the lab, is largely determined by *your* work practices. Always work carefully, use your commonsense, and abide by the safety regulations.

Some important general principles of safe practice are summarized in the following rules

1. *Work carefully, do not take risks.*
   This covers basic rules such as always wearing safety spectacles, never working alone, and working neatly and unhurriedly.

2. *Assess the possible hazards before carrying out a reaction.*
   Find out about the dangers of handling unfamiliar chemicals or apparatus and take note of any necessary precautions.

3. *Know the accident and emergency procedures.*

It is vital to know what to do in case of an accident. This includes being familiar with the fire fighting and first aid equipment, and knowing how to get assistance from qualified personnel.

17.2 Safe working practice

It has been emphasized already that you should be familiar with the regulations and codes of practice pertaining in your laboratory. We will not discuss safety legislation here but some fundamental rules should be stressed. Never work alone in a laboratory. Always wear suitable safety spectacles and a non-flammable lab coat, and use other protection such as gloves, face masks, or safety shields if there is a particular hazard. Never eat, drink or smoke in a laboratory. Work at a safe steady pace, and keep your bench and your lab clean and tidy. Familiarity breeds contempt, do not allow yourself to get careless with everyday dangers such as solvent flammability. Familiarize yourself with the location and operation of the safety equipment in your laboratory.

As regards specific hazards the chief rule is to carry out an assessment of the dangers involved before using an unfamiliar chemical or piece of apparatus. Some of the commonest hazards are described in the next section. Once you are aware of the possible dangers take all the necessary precautions, and ensure that you know what to do if an accident does occur.

Store your chemicals in clearly labelled containers, and abide by the regulations concerning storage of solvents and other hazardous materials. Dispose of waste chemicals safely, according to the approved procedures for your laboratory. Never pour organic compounds down the sink.

17.3 Common hazards

Always assess the risks involved *before* carrying out a reaction. Extensive compilations of information about the dangers posed by a large number of compounds are available (see Bibliography). Consult these references and your supervisor before using a compound or procedure which is new to you. In some areas safety legislation makes it mandatory to conduct such a safety audit, but even if it is not legally required, it should still be regarded as an essential preliminary before doing a reaction.

Remember to treat all compounds, especially new materials, with care. Avoid breathing vapours and do not allow solids or solutions to get on your skin. The majority of accidents are caused by a few common hazards. Some of the most frequently encountered dangers are listed in Table 17.1 and you should be aware of all of these, and always take appropriate precautions. Consult safety manuals and other Sections of this book for more information. Throughout the book safety warnings are highlighted in *bold italic* text.

Table 17.1
Common hazards in the chemical laboratory

Source	Hazard
Glassware	Danger of cuts, leaks of harmful compounds
Solvents	Most are extremely flammable
	Benzene, halogenated solvents are toxic
Vacuum apparatus	May implode violently
Pressure apparatus	May explode violently
Gas cylinders	May leak harmful gases or discharge violently (Chapter 6)
Strong acids	Extremely corrosive
	React violently with water, bases
	May produce harmful vapours
Strong bases	Extremely corrosive
	React violently with acids, protic solvents
Strong oxidizing agents	React violently with easily oxidizable compounds such as organic solvents
Alkali metals	React violently with water, protic solvents and chlorinated solvents
Strong alkylating agents	Extremely toxic

In addition to these general warnings you should be aware of the severe hazards posed by some more specific families of compounds. The compounds listed in Table 17.2 pose a severe risk of explosion and those in Table 17.3 should be regarded as extremely toxic.

Table 17.2

Explosion hazards

Acetylene and metal acetylides

Alkali metals in contact with chlorinated solvents

Azides, both organic and inorganic

Diazo compounds and diazonium salts

Glass vacuum apparatus, e.g. Dewar flasks

Liquid oxygen and liquid air (formed by evaporation of liquid nitrogen)

Nitrates and polynitro compounds, e.g. TNT (trinitrotoluene)

Perchloric acid, perchlorates, and chlorates

Peroxides (formed in ethers and in alkenes on standing in air)

Table 17.3

Toxic and carcinogenic compounds

Compounds of heavy metals (arsenic, mercury, lead, selenium, thallium)

Alkylating agents including methyl iodide, dimethyl sulphate (CARCINOGENIC)

Fluorine, chlorine and bromine

Hydrofluoric acid and metal fluorides

Cyanides and hydrogen cyanide

Oxalic acid and its salts, oxalyl chloride

Aromatic amines and nitro compounds

Ozone

Hydrogen sulphide

Phosgene

Osmium tetroxide

Benzene, polycyclic aromatics (CARCINOGENIC)

Hexamethylphosphoric triamide (HMPA) (CARCINOGENIC)

17.4 Accident and emergency procedures

Regrettably accidents are still all too common so it is vital that you know what to do if an accident does occur. You must be familiar with the fire fighting equipment in your lab (fire extinguishers, fire blankets, sand buckets) and you must know the procedures for summoning the fire brigade and for evacuating the building. In the case of injuries or exposure to harmful chemicals you should know who to summon to administer first aid, and how to get medical assistance. It is particularly important to know how to get help outside of normal working hours. If you are using particularly dangerous materials (such as cyanides) or equipment (such as high pressure apparatus) you should know about the relevant emergency procedures and take precautions such as having antidotes, protective equipment, or qualified personnel at hand. In the aftermath of an accident it is very important that you complete the required accident report forms, and take steps to avoid any possibility of a repeat.

Ask yourself now: are you familiar with accident procedures? If not you should *not* be working in the lab.

17.5 Bibliography

Guide to Safe Practices in Chemical Laboratories, Royal Society of Chemistry, 1986.

Hazards in the Chemical Laboratory, 4th ed., L. Bretherick Ed., Royal Society of Chemistry, 1986.

The Sigma-Aldrich Library of Chemical Safety Data, 2nd ed., R.E. Lenga Ed., Sigma-Aldrich Corp., Milwaukee, 1987.

Dangerous Properties of Industrial Materials, 7th ed., N.I. Sax and R.J. Lewis, Van Nostrand Reinhold Co., New York, 1988.

First Aid Manual for Chemical Accidents, M.J. Lefevre, Dowden Hutchinson and Ross, Stroudsburg, 1980.

Safe Storage of Laboratory Chemicals, D.A. Pipitone, Wiley, New York, 1984.

Handbook of Laboratory Waste Disposal, M.J. Pitt and E. Pitt, Wiley, New York, 1985.

Appendix 1 : Properties of common solvents

Solvent	B.p. (°C)	M.p. (°C)	ε	Density	δ¹H (300MHz, CDCl₃)	δ¹³C (300MHz, CDCl₃)	Preliminary drying	Rigorous drying	TLV (ppm)
Acetic acid	118	17	6.19	1.049	2.08 s, 10-13 br s var	20.7, 177.6	Acetic anhydride	Acetic anhydride	10
Acetone	56	-94	20.7	0.790	2.13 s	30.7, 206.5	3A sieve	3A sieve	1000
Acetonitrile	82	-46	36.2	0.777	1.97 s	1.7, 116.2	Potassium carbonate	Phosphorus pentoxide	40
Benzene	80	5.5	2.28	0.879	7.37 s	128.3	Not necessary	Calcium hydride	10
t-Butanol	82	25	3.49	0.850	1.24 s, 1.35 br s var	31.2, 69.2	Calcium hydride	Calcium hydride	10
Carbon tetrachloride	76	-23	2.23	1.460	-	96.2	Alumina	Phosphorus pentoxide	75
Chlorobenzene	132	-46	5.62	1.106	7.28 br m	126, 129, 130, 134	Not necessary	Calcium hydride	10
Chloroform	62	-63	4.70	1.480	7.24 s	77.0	Alumina	Phosphorus pentoxide	10
Dichloroethane	83	-35	10.4	1.235	3.71 s	44.4	Not necessary	Calcium hydride	10
Dichloromethane	40	-97	8.9	1.325	5.28 s	53.4	Not necessary	Calcium hydride	100
Diethyl ether	35	-116	4.34	0.714	1.18 t, 3.45 q	15.2, 65.8	Calcium chloride; Na	Sodium/benzophenone	400
Dimethoxyethane	83	-58		0.850	3.36 s, 3.51 s	59.0, 71.8	Calcium chloride; Na	Sodium/benzophenone	
Dimethylformamide	152	-61	36.7	0.945	2.81 s, 2.89 s, 7.94 s	31.4, 36.4, 162.4	Calcium hydride	Phosphous pentoxide	10
Dimethyl sulphoxide	189	18	49.0	1.101	2.62 s	40.6	Distillation	4A sieve	
Dioxan	102	12	2.21	1.034	3.66 s	67.0	Calcium chloride: Na	Sodium/benzophenone	50
Ethanol	78	-114	24.3	0.785	1.18 t, 2.05 br s, 3.65q	18.3, 58.2	Magnesium	3A sieve	1000
Ethyl acetate	77	-84	6.02	0.900	1.22 t, 2.01 s, 4.09 q	14.1,20.9,60.3,171.0	Potassium carbonate	4A sieve	400
HMPA	235	7		1.030	2.59 d	36.8	Calcium hydride	Calcium hydride	200
Methanol	64	-97	32.6	0.791	1.94 br s var, 3.42 s	50.5	Magnesium	3A sieve	200
Nitromethane	101	-28	38.6	1.137	4.33 s	62.4	Calcium chloride	4A sieve	100
Pyridine	116	-42	12.3	0.982	7.24 m, 7.63 m, 8.58 m	123.6, 135.8, 149.8	Calcium hydride	Calcium hydride	5
Tetrahydrofuran	66	-65	18.5	0.805	1.82 m, 3.72 m	25.6, 67.9	Calcium chloride; Na	Sodium/benzophenone	200
Toluene	111	-95	2.38	0.867	2.32 s, 7.17 br s	21,125,128,129,138	Not necessary	Calcium hydride	100
Water	100	0	78.5	1.000					

Appendix 2 : Properties of common gases

Gas	Mol. weight	B.p.[a]	M.p.[b]	Density of gas[c]	Density of liquid[d]	Hazardous properties[e]	TLV[f]
Acetylene	26.04	-84		1.109		As, Fl, Note g	25
Ammonia	17.03	-33	-78	0.71	0.68	To, Co, Fl	
Argon	39.944	-189	-186	1.66	1.4	As	
Boron trichloride	117.19	12.5	-107	4.85		To, Co	
Boron trifluoride	67.81	-100	-127	3	1.59	To, Co	1
Carbon dioxide	44.01		-78	1.83		Co	5000
Carbon monoxide	28.01	-191	-207	1.16	0.79	To, Fl	50
Chlorine	70.914	-34	-101	2.97	1.56	To, Co	1
Ethylene	28.05	-104	-170	1.17	0.57	Fl	
Ethylene oxide	44.05	10.7	-112	1.82	0.88	To, Fl	5
Fluorine	37.997	-188	-220	1.57	1.5	Fl, Co	1
Helium	4.0026	-269	-272	0.17	0.12	As	
Hydrogen	2.016	-253		0.08	0.07	Fl	
Hydrogen bromide	80.917	-67	-87	3.34	2.16	To, Co	3
Hydrogen chloride	36.461	-85	-114	1.52	1.19	To, Co	5
Hydrogen fluoride	20.006	19.5	-83	0.94	1.0	To, Co	3
Hydrogen sulphide	34.08	-60	-85	1.43		To, Co, Fl	10
Isobutylene	56.11	-6.9	-140	2.39	0.63	Fl	
Methanethiol	48.107	6	-121	2.14	0.89	To, Fl	0.5
Nitric oxide (NO)	30.006	-152	-164	1.24	1.27	To	25
Nitrogen	28.0134	-196		1.25	0.8	As	
Nitrogen dioxide (NO₂)	46.0055	21	-9.3	3.3	1.45	To, Co	3
Oxygen	32.0	-183	-218	1.33	1.14	Ox	
Phosgene	98.92	8.2	-128	4.1	1.41	To, Co	0.1
Sulphur dioxide	64.063	-10	-75	2.70	1.46	To, Co	2

Notes

a. °C at 1 atm
b. °C
c. g/l at 20°C at 1 atm
d. g/ml at b.p.
e. As = Asphyxiant
    Co = Corrosive
    Fl = Flammable
    Ox = Oxidising
    To = Toxic
f. ppm
g. Potentially explosive when pressurised

Appendix 3 : Approximate* pKa values for some common deprotonations cf. some common bases

Reagent to be deprotonated	pKa	Bases	pKa (of BH)
ArSH	7		
RCH$_2$NO$_2$	9		
RCOCH$_2$CN	9		
RCOCH$_2$COR	9		
RSH	10	Et$_3$N	11
RCOCH$_2$CO$_2$R	11	Et$_2$NH	11
RCO$_2$CH$_2$CO$_2$R	13		
Cyclopentadiene	15	Na$^+$ $^-$OH	16
RCH$_2$CHO	17	Na$^+$ $^-$OEt	18
RC≡CH	25	K$^+$ $^-$OtBu	19
CH$_3$COCH$_3$	20		
CH$_3$CO$_2$Et	25	Na$^+$ $^-$H	35
CH$_3$CN	25	Na$^+$ $^-$NH$_2$	35
PhH	41	Li$^+$ $^-$NiPr$_2$	36
H$_2$C=CHCH$_3$	43		
H$_2$C=CH$_2$	44	Li$^+$ $^-$nBu	50
		Li$^+$ $^-$tBu	>50

*These figures are very approximate. A pKa difference of >4 between base and reagent will cause complete deprotonation.

Appendix 4 : Lewis acids

Lewis acid	Compatible solvents	Comments
Aluminium trichloride	Hydrocarbons, halogenated	Strong, widely used in Friedel-Crafts
Boron tribromide	Hydrocarbons, halogenated	Strong, used to cleave ethers, acetals
Boron trichloride	Hydrocarbons, halogenated	Strong, used to cleave ethers, acetals
Boron trifluoride etherate	Many solvents	Moderate, very versatile
Diethylaluminium chloride	Hydrocarbons, halogenated	Moderate, useful for proton-sensitive reactions
Ethylaluminium dichloride	Hydrocarbons, halogenated	Moderate, useful for proton-sensitive reactions
Ferric chloride	Hydrocarbons, halogenated	Moderate
Mercuric chloride	Many solvents	Weak, useful for cleaving C-S bonds
Lanthanide shift reagents	Many solvents	Weak, useful for reactions involving sensitive dienes, ethers
Magnesium bromide	Hydrocarbons, halogenated	Moderate
Magnesium chloride.etherate	Hydrocarbons, halogenated, ethers	Moderate
Silver chloride	Many solvents	Moderate, used to generate carbonium ions
Silver triflate	Many solvents	Moderate, used to generate carbonium ions
Stannic chloride	Hydrocarbons, halogenated	Strong, very versatile
Titanium tetrachloride	Hydrocarbons, halogenated	Strong, very versatile
Trimethylsilyl iodide	Hydrocarbons, halogenated, MeCN	Strong, used to cleave ethers, acetals, esters
Trimethylsilyl triflate	Hydrocarbons, halogenated	Strong, used with silylated reagents
Zinc bromide	Hydrocarbons, halogenated	Moderate, versatile
Zinc chloride	Hydrocarbons, halogenated, ethers	Moderate, versatile

Appendix 5 : Common reducing reagents

1. Hydride reducing agents

Reagent	Typical solvents	Temperature (°C)	Functional groups reduced
LiBH$_4$ (lithium borohydride)	Tetrahydrofuran	0 to RT	ester → alcohol ketone → alcohol aldehyde → alcohol
Li[Et$_3$BH] (Superhydride) (lithium triethylborohydride)	Tetrahydrofuran	-78 to RT	ester → alcohol ketone → alcohol aldehyde → alcohol alkyl halide → alkane epoxide → alcohol
Li[^{s}Bu$_3$BH] (L-Selectride) (lithium tri-*sec*-butylborohydride)	Tetrahydrofuran	-78 to RT	ketone → alcohol aldehyde → alcohol alkyl halide → alkane
NaBH$_4$ (sodium borohydride)	Alcohols, ethers	0 to RT	ketone → alcohol aldehyde → alcohol
Na[BH$_3$CN] (sodium cyanoborohydride)	Alcohols, water, DMSO	0 to RT	ketone → alcohol aldehyde → alcohol alkyl halide → alkane imine → amine
Na[BH(OAc)$_3$] (sodium triacetoxyborohydride)	Acetic acid	0 to RT	ketone → alcohol aldehyde → alcohol

Appendix 5 cont'd

Reagent	Typical solvents	Temperature (°C)	Functional groups reduced
$Zn(BH_4)_2$ (zinc borohydride)	Ethers	0 to RT	ketone → alcohol aldehyde → alcohol
$^nBu_4NBH_4$ (tetra-n-butylammonium borohydride)	Dichloromethane, ethers	0 to RT	ketone → alcohol aldehyde → alcohol
$LiAlH_4$ (lithium aluminium hydride)	Ethers	-78 to RT	ester → alcohol ketone → alcohol aldehyde → alcohol alkyl halide → alkane acetylene → trans alkene epoxide → alcohol imine → amine amide → amine
$Li[(^tBuO)_3AlH]$ (lithium tri-tert-butoxyaluminium hydride)	Tetrahydrofuran	-78 RT	acid chloride → aldehyde ketone → alcohol aldehyde → alcohol
$Na[AlH_2(OCH_2CH_2OCH_3)_2]$ (RED-AL) (sodium bis-[2-methoxyethoxy]-aluminium hydride)	Ethers, toluene	-78 to RT	ester → alcohol ketone → alcohol aldehyde → alcohol alkyl halide → alkane epoxide → alcohol α,β-unsaturated enone → allylic alcohol

Appendix 5 cont'd

Reagent	Solvent	Temperature	Reactions
B_2H_6 (diborane)	Dichloromethane, tetrahydrofuran	-78 to RT, RT	carboxylic acid → alcohol, amide → amine, ketone → alcohol, aldehyde → alcohol
$BH_3S(CH_3)_2$ (borane-dimethylsulphide complex)	Tetrahydrofuran, dimethyl sulphide	-78 to RT, RT	carboxylic acid → alcohol, amide → amine, ketone → alcohol, aldehyde → alcohol
$(Sia)_2BH$ (disiamylborane)	Tetrahydrofuran	-78 to RT	ketone → alcohol, aldehyde → alcohol, lactone → lactol
AlH_3 (alane)	Ethers	-78 to RT	ester → alcohol, ketone → alcohol, aldehyde → alcohol, alkyl halide → alkane, epoxide → alcohol, lactone → cyclic ether
$^iBu_2AlH$ (DIBAL) (Di-isobutylaluminium hydride)	Dichloromethane, ethers, toluene	-78, -78 to RT	ester → aldehyde, lactone → lactol, amide → aldehyde, nitrile → aldehyde, ketone → alcohol, aldehyde → alcohol, α,β-unsaturated ketone → allylic alcohol, acetylene → cis-alkene

Appendix 5 cont'd

2. Single electron transfer reducing agents

Reagent	Typical Solvents	Temperature (°C)	Functional Groups Reduced
Li/NH$_3$ (lithium in ammonia)	Liquid ammonia	-78 -78 to -33	α,β-unsaturated ketone → ketone ketone → alcohol aldehyde → alcohol aryl ring → dihydroaryl ring
LiC$_{10}$H$_8$ (lithium naphthalenide)	Tetrahydrofuran	-78 to RT	sulphide → alkane sulphone → alkane
NaHg (sodium amalgam)	Methanol	0-RT	ketone → alcohol aldehyde → alcohol sulphone → alkane

3. Common hydrogenation catalysts

Catalyst	Solvent	Temperature (°C)	H$_2$ Pressure (bar)	Functional Groups Reduced
Ni	Alcohols, toluene	5 to 100	3-10	alkene → alkane ketone → alcohol aldehyde → alcohol
Pd/C	Alcohols Alcohols, acetic acid Toluene	5 to 50 5 to 100 5 to 100	1-5 1-10 1-10	aromatic nitro → aromatic amine nitrile → amine acetylene → alkane alkyl halide → alkane

Appendix 5 cont'd

Catalyst	Solvent			Reaction
Pd/BaSO$_4$	Alcohols, toluene	5 to 100	3-10	alkene → alkane
	Toluene	50 to 150	3-50	imines → amine
	Acetic acid			alkyl nitro → amine
				epoxide → alcohol
Pt/C	Alcohols, toluene	5 to 50	1-3	acetylene → cis alkene
	Alcohols	5 to 50	1-5	aromatic nitro → aromatic amine
	Alcohols, toluene	5 to 100	3-10	olefin → alkane
				ketone → alcohol
				aldehyde → alcohol
	Toluene	50 to 150	3-50	α,β-unsaturated ketone → alylic alcohol
				imines → amine
Rh/C	Alcohols, toluene	5 to 100	3-10	olefin → alkane
	Acetic acid, alcohols	50 to 150	3-50	aromatic ring → cyclohexane
				ketone → alcohol
				aldehyde → alcohol
Rh/Al$_2$O$_3$	Alcohols	50 to 150	3-50	aromatic ring → cyclohexane

Appendix 6 :   Common oxidizing reagents

Reagent	Typical Solvents	Temperature (°C)	Functional Groups Oxidized
CrO_3/H_2SO_4 (H_2CrO_4) (Jones reagent; chromic acid)	Acetone; ether	0 to RT	2° alcohol→ ketone 1° alcohol→ acid aldehyde → alcohol
$CrO_3.Py_2$ (Collins reagent)	Pyridine;dichloromethane	0 to RT	2° alcohol→ ketone 1° alcohol→ aldehyde
$PyH^+CrO_3Cl^-$ (PCC) (pyridinium chlorochromate)	Dichloromethane; DMF	0 to RT	2° alcohol→ ketone 1° alcohol→ aldehyde
$(PyH^+)_2Cr_2O_7$ (PDC) (pyridinium dichromate)	Dichloromethane; DMF	0 to RT	2° alcohol→ ketone 1° alcohol→ aldehyde
Ag_2CO_3/Celite (Fetizon's reagent) (silver carbonate on Celite)	Hexane; benzene; chloroform	RT, Reflux	2° alcohol→ ketone diols→lactones
MnO_2 (manganese dioxide)	Hexane; benzene; dichloromethane	0, RT, Reflux	selective for allylic or benzylic alcohols→ aldehydes or ketones
$KMnO_4$ (potassium permanganate)	Often used in aqueous solution	0, RT, reflux	Very powerful oxidant 2° alcohol→ ketone 1° alcohol→ acid

Appendix 6 cont'd

KMnO$_4$ cont'd			alkene→diol sulphide→ sulphone
RuO$_4$	Carbon tetrachloride/ acetonitrile/water	RT	cleaves alkenes → carboxylic acids
Al(OR)$_3$/Me$_2$CO (Oppenauer oxidation) Al(OR)$_3$/cyclohexanone	Acetone; toluene	RT Reflux	2° alcohol→ ketone
Pb(OAc)$_4$ (lead tetraacetate)	Benzene; acetic acid; acetonitrile	-78 to RT	cleaves 1,2 diols → C=O compounds ketones→ α-acetoxy-ketones many other systems also oxidized
DMSO/electrophilic reagent (El.) El. = (COCl)$_2$ (oxalyl chloride) /Et$_3$N DCC (dicyclohexylcarbodiimide) (CF$_3$CO)$_2$O (trifluroacetic acid anhydride) Py.SO$_3$ (pyridine-sulphur trioxide)	Dichloromethane Dichloromethane Dichloromethane Dichloromethane DMSO	-40 to RT	2° alcohol→ ketone 1° alcohol→ aldehyde
N-Chlorosuccinimide (NCS)/Me$_2$S (DMS) (N-Chlorosuccinimide/dimethyl sulphide)	Toluene	-20	2° alcohol→ ketone 1° alcohol→ aldehyde

Appendix 6 cont'd

Reagent	Typical Solvents	Temperature (°C)	Functional Groups Oxidized
OsO₄/N-methylmorpholine-N-oxide (NMO) (osmium tetroxide/ N-methylmorpholine-N-oxide)	Acetone/water; t-butanol	RT	alkene→ 1,2-diol
OsO₄/NaIO₄ (osmium tetroxide/sodium periodate)	Ether/water; dioxan/water	RT	cleaves alkenes→ C=O compounds
m-Chloroperoxybenzoic acid (MCPBA)	Dichloromethane	-20 to RT	alkene→ epoxide sulphide→ sulphoxide/sulphone
Ti(OPrⁱ)₄/BuᵗOOH/tartrate ester (Sharpless oxidation) (titanium isopropoxide/t-butyl hydroperoxide/ dialkyl tartrate)	Dichloromethane	-20	enantioselective epoxidation of allylic alcohols
VO(acac)₂/BuᵗOOH (vanadyl acetylacetonate/t-butyl hydroperoxide)	Dichloromethane	-20 to RT	allylic alcohols→ epoxides
H₂O₂/PhCH₂(Me)₃N⁺ OH⁻ (hydrogen peroxide/benzyltrimethyl-ammonium hydroxide)	Alcohols	0 to RT	α,β-unsaturated C=O→ epoxide
PdCl₂/CuCl₂/O₂ (Wacker oxidation) (palladium chloride/cupric chloride/oxygen)	Sulpholane/water	RT to 100	terminal alkenes→ methyl ketones

Appendix 6 cont'd

Pt/O₂ (platinum/oxygen)	Acetone/water	RT to 100	1° alcohol → acid diol → lactone
O₃ (ozone)	Dichloromethane; methanol	-78 to RT	cleaves alkenes → carbonyl compounds

Index